About This Book

Why is this topic important?

This is the first book exclusively dedicated to helping HR professionals manage their careers throughout their entire working lives. This book is important in that over a million people who identify themselves with the HR profession have had no comprehensive guide to their own careers and the choices they will make throughout their working lives. There are plenty of books about how to manage human resources, but this is the first book on how to manage the HR profession itself.

What can you achieve with this book?

This book helps you understand how to manage your HR career *over time.* By providing you with important insights into how HR success is made (and how mistakes can be avoided), this book is the only guide to the HR profession from start to finish—and beyond. You will learn:

- How to position yourself to be qualified and competitive for career-building opportunities throughout your working life.
- How to create a fantastic HR career on purpose, not by happenstance.
- How to create your own luck.
- How to leverage less-than-optimal situations to position yourself for your next big career growth spurt.
- How to have as much control as possible over the variables that will inevitably infiltrate your career.
- How to eliminate the most painful regret of them all: That you weren't ready when your dream opportunity came along.

How is this book organized?

Eight chapters lay out the entire landscape of HR career choices for readers who want to achieve their full potential and ambitions in human resource management. Exclusive one-on-one interviews with HR stars about how they developed their careers are interspersed between chapters. By the time you finish this book, the mysteries of the HR career path will be replaced by a solid career plan that you can develop for yourself.

About Pfeiffer

Pfeiffer serves the professional development and hands-on resource needs of training and human resource practitioners and gives them products to do their jobs better. We deliver proven ideas and solutions from experts in HR development and HR management, and we offer effective and customizable tools to improve workplace performance. From novice to seasoned professional, Pfeiffer is the source you can trust to make yourself and your organization more successful.

Essential Knowledge Pfeiffer produces insightful, practical, and comprehensive materials on topics that matter the most to training and HR professionals. Our Essential Knowledge resources translate the expertise of seasoned professionals into practical, how-to guidance on critical workplace issues and problems. These resources are supported by case studies, worksheets, and job aids and are frequently supplemented with CD-ROMs, websites, and other means of making the content easier to read, understand, and use.

Essential Tools Pfeiffer's Essential Tools resources save time and expense by offering proven, ready-to-use materials—including exercises, activities, games, instruments, and assessments—for use during a training or team-learning event. These resources are frequently offered in looseleaf or CD-ROM format to facilitate copying and customization of the material.

Pfeiffer also recognizes the remarkable power of new technologies in expanding the reach and effectiveness of training. While e-hype has often created whizbang solutions in search of a problem, we are dedicated to bringing convenience and enhancements to proven training solutions. All our e-tools comply with rigorous functionality standards. The most appropriate technology wrapped around essential content yields the perfect solution for today's on-the-go trainers and human resource professionals.

Essential resources for training and HR professionals

THE HUMAN RESOURCE PROFESSIONAL'S CAREER GUIDE

THE HUMAN RESOURCE PROFESSIONAL'S CAREER GUIDE

Building a Position of Strength

Jeanne Palmer

with Martha I. Finney

•

Published by Pfeiffer
An Imprint of Wiley
989 Market Street, San Francisco, CA 94103-1741 www.pfeiffer.com

For additional copies/bulk purchases of this book in the U.S. please contact 800-274-4434.

Pfeiffer books and products are available through most bookstores. To contact Pfeiffer directly call our Customer Care Department within the U.S. at 800-274-4434, outside the U.S. at 317-572-3985, fax 317-572-4002, or visit www.pfeiffer.com.

Pfeiffer also publishes its books in a variety of electronic formats. Some content that appears in print may not be available in electronic books.

Library of Congress Cataloging-in-Publication Data

Palmer, Jeanne, date
The human resource professional's career guide: building a position of strength / Jeanne Palmer with Martha I. Finney.
p. cm.
Includes index.
ISBN 0-7879-7331-9 (alk. paper)
1. Personnel management—Vocational guidance. 2. Career development. I. Finney, Martha I. II. Title.
HF5549.5.C35P356 2004
658.3'0023—dc22

2003028272

Acquiring Editor: Matthew Davis
Director of Development: Kathleen Dolan Davies
Developmental Editor: Susan Rachmeler

Production Editor: Nina Kreiden
Editor: Rebecca Taff
Manufacturing Supervisor: Bill Matherly
Illustrations: Richard Sheppard Illustration

Printed in the United States of America
Printing 10 9 8 7 6 5 4 3 2 1

CONTENTS

To my parents—my Mom, who gave me the strength and fortitude to persevere, and my Dad, who gave me the wisdom to look beyond; to my husband and sons, whose love and support I could not survive without.

Jeanne Palmer

ACKNOWLEDGMENTS

I HAVE ALWAYS told myself and others that "I'd rather be lucky than smart" because I have always considered myself lucky. I guess that is just another way of saying I feel blessed. Somehow, in the end, I truly believe things have a way of working out the way they are supposed to. That being said, one of the things I feel luckiest about is the many people who are important parts of my life—those who have been there for me, and I do hope I have been there for them—my family, friends, and colleagues. To mention just a few:

- The Palmer Advantage team—always with a sense of humor
- Our many clients—who demand the best of us all of the time
- Our numerous candidates—who are patient, understanding, and willing to share their experiences in honest, open ways
- The University of California Santa Cruz Extension—where I have learned so much and been able to touch so many
- The vice presidents of human resources who have been willing to share their insights and experiences with the world
- Martha Finney—who provided an immense amount of guidance and expertise in the writing of this book
- Matt Davis for his support, advice, and vision

San Jose, California
April 2004

JEANNE PALMER

INTRODUCTION: GETTING THE MOST FROM THIS RESOURCE

SOMEWHERE OUT THERE your perfect next job exists. The right company. The right compensation. The right next step. The right location. The right everything.

There's only one problem: At the moment, someone else has that job. *At the moment.*

Let's say his name is Jack. This is no longer Jack's perfect job, and he's ready to move on. And he's done everything right. So, one day, while he's focusing on his work, his phone rings. Suddenly he's being offered the job of his dreams and, after a dignified amount of time to deliberate (or at least appear to), he accepts the great new opportunity and gives notice.

Suddenly your perfect job is available! Jack's former boss gets together with *her* boss, maybe a search committee, maybe a headhunter. As a group they hammer out the specifications for the new opening, and it has your name written all over it. In a manner of speaking, that is.

Does your phone ring? Do they even know you're alive? Let's say they don't. And that perfect job that you're the perfect candidate for goes to someone else. The employer must settle for second best because the search team doesn't know about you. And you never hear about the job at all. And when the time comes for you to look for a new job, you begin with this uncomfortable flat-footed feeling that maybe you're a little too far along in your career to be sending résumés to blind want ads, post office boxes, or those black-hole Internet job boards—or to recruiters. And you wonder if you're going to have to settle for a less-than-perfect new opportunity—an opportunity that would actually have been perfect for someone else, who, in turn has now had to settle for a less-than-perfect position.

Or . . . here's a happier scenario. Jack gets that fabulous new job offer and resigns, leaving his wonderful job open. His boss gets together with the search team, hammers out the specs, and the recruiter says, "I know just the right person!"

And a few hours later, your phone rings. And in a few short weeks, you're telling your friends, "It was amazing. I wasn't even looking for a new job, and this perfect opportunity landed right in my lap! Just dumb luck, I guess."

Or was it?

In my more than thirty years in and about HR, first as a practitioner, and then in the last ten years recruiting exclusively for HR positions, I am repeatedly reminded how even the best, most talented, most experienced HR professionals are at a loss when it comes to managing their own careers. It's counterintuitive, I know. You would think that those very people who are tasked with the responsibility of running the people side of business and—in turn—helping their employees develop themselves professionally, would be masters at driving their own career destinies. So don't feel bad about yourself if you're thinking that maybe you're not on as high-potential a track as you thought you would be by now. You're not alone.

There are several reasons why the HR career path has been mysterious territory until now:

1. The HR career can be vague, highly subjective, and even politically charged. It's a highly complex field with many opportunities for entry, many paths to the top, and, unfortunately, many opportunities to fail utterly.
2. In HR, you can come up from a variety of different backgrounds. You can even enter HR from an entirely different business discipline (we'll get to that later on in the book).
3. Your constituencies aren't always clear in HR. So it's not always easy to know what success looks like. We've all heard the question: Who's HR's customer? (It's the basic chicken/egg riddle of HR that fills seminars or can keep a cocktail party going into the wee hours.) The expectations of your performance (and results) aren't always the same, or even clear. In finance, it's predictable. In sales, it's predictable. In marketing, it's predictable. Those folks know what success looks like. And, by and large, most people inside the organization appreciate how people in those departments contribute to the company's goals. But the HR function's responsibilities span the organization, across all other functions in the organization. A single HR result could have winners and losers within the same company creating situations that will not necessarily endear HR to everyone in the organization. The HR department is sometimes the function that employees love to hate. And this can be very distracting, even upsetting, to HR professionals, especially those who were drawn to the profession because they see themselves as *people* people.

4. HR professionals are busy trying to meet this diverse set of demands and are frequently focused on elevating the stature of the profession within their companies. Could it be that they're so busy taking care of the careers of others that they neglect their own? Or they're so busy focusing on the organization and daily business fires that they simply forget that great careers don't just happen?
5. There are many mixed messages out there. Get an MBA. Don't get an MBA; get an advanced human resources degree instead. Be "strictly business," bottom-line oriented. Don't forget you're about the people. Should you stay more than five years? Or should you jump ship the minute a better opportunity comes along? And how do you handle all those nuisance calls from headhunters who want to steal your employees—or build their business through you? Are you nice to them? Or do you tell them to buzz off? If you keep them at arm's length so you can focus on *your* business, will they ever call with opportunities for *you*?
6. Frankly, there isn't a lot out there that maps out dynamic career paths for ambitious HR professionals. Up until the 2003 release of *HR from the Heart,* written by Libby Sartain with my co-author Martha I. Finney, there were no books even approaching the subject of how to build a world-class HR career. All the HR-specific books up to that point were about how to do the job, not how to cultivate a life's work, a career that progresses and grows as *you* progress and grow.

No matter who you are, what your education or experience may be, or how far along you are in your career, you can control your career prospects and realign your path to more closely match your ambition and potential. Your career and prospects are entirely within your control. It's all in knowing how.

IS THIS BOOK FOR YOU?

Martha and I wrote this book specifically to provide both inspiration and practical information for readers at almost every stage of their careers, just short of achieving the top-most seat in HR. This book will be useful to readers still in college and planning the first phases of their careers all the way to mid-level professionals aspiring to achieve the top-most level of their working lives, whether it be corporate senior vice president of HR or director of a specialty area.

No matter where you are in your profession, the combination of practical advice from an executive recruiter and one-on-one, in-depth interviews with HR stars will give you everything you need to know to become an HR star in your own right.

IF YOU ONLY CHASE NEW CAREER OPPORTUNITIES, YOU'LL NEVER GET AHEAD

Think of your best career future as a moving target. Marksmen will tell you that the way to hit a moving target is to *get in front of it,* not chase it down. Your experience, abilities, and reputation must already be there when your next ideal career opportunity finds you, not the other way around.

Unfortunately, as a recruiter for HR positions, I've seen thousands of perfectly well-qualified candidates chase down the opportunities, only to have those golden chances slip from their grasp. They weren't prepared. They were too negative or jaded about their career life story. Or worse: There was no story to their career at all. No one had ever heard of them or their companies. They were unable to articulate what they had accomplished, the impact they were able to have or the decisions they were able to influence. Or they couldn't speak cogently about who they are, what they stand for, or where they want to be in the next five, ten, fifteen, or twenty years. They're constantly *behind* their mark, never catching up.

In this book, Martha and I have gathered the best advice from my own files and the personal experiences of some of the most successful HR stars out there to help you get *in front* of your career trajectory. That way the right people will be making your phone ring with the right job opportunities. Again and again! Even when you're not actively looking. And you'll be prepared to take the next big step that continues a unique success story that you have already begun writing.

YOU HAVE MORE CONTROL OVER YOUR CAREER THAN YOU THINK YOU DO

By the time you finish this book, the mysteries of the HR career path will be replaced by a solid career plan that you'll be able to develop for yourself. You will

- Know how to position yourself to get the calls that are right for you!

- Know how to create a career on purpose, not by happenstance.
- Know how to create your own luck.
- Know how to leverage less-than-optimal situations to position yourself for your next big career growth spurt.
- Know how to have as much control as possible over the variables that will inevitably infiltrate your career.
- Know how to eliminate the most painful regret of them all: That you weren't ready when your dream opportunity came along.

Even in hard economic times, there are still plenty of terrific HR openings that need to be filled. The problem isn't that there are not enough jobs to go around; the biggest problem all professional recruiters have is not having enough high-quality candidates to deliver to their clients. By the time corporate clients come to recruiters, they want extraordinary and specific candidates—the kind they know they can't find on their websites, or even in such high-end Help Wanteds as those found in *The Wall Street Journal* or the business sections of *The New York Times.* These clients are looking for people with a specific set of experiences and skills. *And they're looking for people who aren't looking for them.*

You want to be among the ranks of those stars who are sought after, not the ones soaking up their Sunday mornings surrounded by newspaper classifieds and yellow highlighters. You want to be the one with the choices.

If you are just beginning your career, you may be thinking that this ideal scenario is too far away for you to be worrying about right now. But now is the perfect time for you to build a long-term HR career plan and path with purpose and direction, yet flexible enough to transform and grow as your own ambitions mature and you become more confident in your abilities.

Yes, your HR career will always be filled with judgment calls, subjective moments, and those people issues that seemed to be filled with emotion more than business strategy.

That's what it means to be in HR. But when it comes to creating a rewarding and challenging HR career over time, you don't have to feel your way.

Not anymore.

HOW THIS BOOK IS DIFFERENT

As we've already established, this book is the first book to deal exclusively in the care, planning, and development of your HR career. This is not a generic career management book. If you're an engineer and want to stay in engineering, this book isn't for you.

This book is also about how to cultivate your HR career *over time.* I can't promise you that the information in this book will get you your "next job in ten days." But I can promise you that after you've passed your immediate emergency mode, the information and inspiration contained in these pages can help you avoid being in an urgent job search mode ever again. While Martha and I do offer suggestions on how to break into HR, and we do offer some advice on how to make the most of your interview experiences, we've written this book assuming that you know (or can find out on your own) the basic nuts and bolts of interviewing for and landing a job.

Once you have chosen the human resources field for your long-term career, this book will help you map out the rest of your career for the rest of your life. It will give you the step-by-step instructions on how to achieve your ultimate dream for your HR career, whether you want to be the top people chief in a multi-billion-dollar company by the time you're forty-five, or you know that your ideal top spot is to be director of staffing, or you cherish the dream of quickly becoming a consultant providing human resource services to small to mid-sized companies.

HOW THIS BOOK IS ORGANIZED

Chapter 1: "Yes" Is a Success That Doesn't Happen by Accident

In this chapter you will discover the core competencies and key characteristics that make HR professionals irresistible to executive recruiters and high-potential employers. I also introduce you to the concept of career kitting, which will encourage you to take a fresh look at your skills and experiences to determine which choices you may want to make in the next year, five years, ten years, and throughout your working life.

Chapter 2: Every Choice Tells a Story

You may have an outstanding career, with all the essential skills and experiences you need to rise to the very top of your ambition. But you must be able to tell the stories behind all your choices and accomplishments to convince recruiters and search committees that you are their best choice. The chapter lays out the landscape of the various roles HR plays inside the corporate structure and teaches you how to both lay out your long-term career plan and keep track of your accomplishments so that you can use them to illustrate examples of your value as a business partner.

Chapter 3: The Power of the Planned Transition

How you transition from one job to the next opportunity can be just as significant to your long-term career prospects as the new opportunity you're going to. This chapter tells you how to plan your next step as much as a full year ahead of your desired transition time, and how to take care of the relationships that will re-enter your life again and again as the years go by.

Chapter 4: "Hey, I Know Someone . . .": How to Make the Market Come to You

All the HR stars know that the best job opportunities come to them via word-of-mouth, relationships, and reputation. They don't go out actively seeking jobs. Their phones ring with opportunities regularly. This chapter describes how you can build a powerful network of career-building contacts to make your phone ring too—with opportunities to consider and interview for jobs you won't be able to find published in the newspaper or on-line.

Chapter 5: Recover from Your Missteps

If you're in human resources and you're going to be challenging yourself and taking the risks necessary to develop your future, you will make a misstep or two or six. Take heart: You can recover from your mistakes. This chapter tells you how to take the sting out of your regret or embarrassment and keep building your career toward the future.

Chapter 6: Control What You Can; Let the Rest Go

Even with your newfound philosophy of empowerment and perspective, there will still be a moment or two in your career when you absolutely have no power over the outcome. This chapter helps you come to terms with those things you can't change, as well as helps you take essential steps to at least mitigate some of the hazards to your long-term career prospects.

Chapter 7: The Interview Process: How to Handle the Hot Seat

As you become more senior in your career, you'll notice significant changes in the interview process. Recruiters and search committees will still be interested in what you know and what you have done. But they're also going to be increasingly interested in how you can help them achieve the company's objectives and goals. This chapter will help you understand the changing nature of senior-level interviews.

Chapter 8: Prepare Yourself for a Future You Can't Imagine Today

As we've learned over recent years, it's impossible to predict what is going to happen in the future. Anyone old enough to read this book has already experienced many changes in his or her corporate and career world. To achieve your long-term career goals, you must be prepared to shift and change as the economy changes, as your industry changes, as world affairs cause change everywhere. This chapter tells you how to prepare for unexpected changes that will spell new opportunities for those who are flexible, resilient, and aware.

Between chapters we've included one or two exclusive interviews with the top HR executives in some of the most exciting companies in the United States. Their stories, observations, and lessons, in their own voices, paint a full picture of the saga that makes up an HR career over a lifetime. In each interview the HR stars have wonderfully different answers to such questions as:

- What is the best piece of advice you ever received?
- What is the moment at which your career changed forever?
- What is the one thing you wish you had done differently?
- What is the best piece of advice you have to offer someone on the way up?
- What is the best thing newcomers to the profession can do for themselves?
- What's the worst?

We have also included two appendices in the back of the book that will give you a quick map of how the various HR career paths are laid out, according to qualifications necessary to achieve your goals. You'll find the websites listed in Appendix B to be very valuable as you decide to further your education and increase your networking activities.

TERMINOLOGY

And finally, a short note about our shorthand expression: "A Players." Martha and I decided to use this term as a way to indicate the "best of the best." One of our interviewees, Ann Rhoades, shared her definition of "A Players" with us. This is what she had to say: "A Players participate actively in an organization. They're not afraid for their jobs ever. They will step forward when everyone else is stepping back—often at great risk to their careers. They aren't focused on just their area; they have a bigger picture of the organization. A Players care more about how what they do contributes to the entire organization, not just their immediate world. And A Players make companies A Player companies, because A Players attract other A Players. Pretty soon, you'll have a company full of them."

No matter where you are in your career right now, over time you can make yourself an A Player as well.

This book will help you realize that ambition.

1

"YES" IS A SUCCESS THAT DOESN'T JUST HAPPEN BY ACCIDENT

This chapter outlines ways you can take strategic control over your career by dispassionately assessing how your skills and experiences align with the expectations of high-potential hiring companies. Whether the economy is healthy or faltering, there are always highly desirable opportunities in HR.

IS THERE ANY WONDER why the human resource career path is one of the most mysterious inside the corporate world? Human resources (HR) as a function is still obsessively trying to identify and quantify once and for all its financial, strategic, and operational advantage to the organization—that ever-elusive *return on investment* (ROI). If we still haven't definitively decided for ourselves what makes a valuable HR *department,* it's only natural that we haven't yet thoroughly come to understand what makes a powerful, leadership-bound HR *career*—a career in which, over time, you assume greater responsibilities and opportunities to contribute to your company's success on important, strategic levels and a career in which you're recognized and rewarded well for those contributions. Your ambitions will ultimately take you to the highest levels of your career in organizations where your skills, talent, passion, and knowledge will be put into full use to make a strategic difference to the organizations you're associated with and provide you with the career satisfaction and financial rewards you desire.

The same outcomes that an HR professional can offer an organization have parallel qualities and experiences that will make one HR career successful over another. The trouble is that organizations are still trying to figure out what they want from HR. Consequently, the HR profession is still trying to figure out what core qualifications, experiences, and insights will make its key practitioners stars. And, as individuals, we're trying to figure out what we dare hope for ourselves—if only our abilities and talents can match our ambition and vision for our future. We're all learning as we go along.

Likewise, as companies are becoming increasingly clear about what they expect and need from HR—and the best companies in the world are getting closer and closer to that goal—they will be increasingly looking for HR leaders who already know what they're about! And this is the one weakness that we HR recruiters experience in our candidates over and over again. Many HR candidates, even those with brilliant résumés, don't know how brilliant they are. Or if they do, they don't know how to discuss and describe what they can do in irresistible terms that make them the obvious choice for the hiring company.

And here's the worst news of all: The recruiter probably won't tell you how or why you failed to receive that offer that was perfect for you, the one that could have brought your career to the next level! If you're lucky, recruiters may coach you in advance of the interview to help you bring out your best. But once the "no" comes down from the hiring committee, the recruiters are on to coaching the next likely candidate, always aiming for a "yes" that's perfect for both the individual and the client company. The job of the recruiter isn't to help you find a job. The job of the recruiter is to help the client company find the ideal candidate. So once you are passed over, back your résumé goes into the vast files inside the recruiter's database. How soon your résumé resurfaces will depend on how soon the recruiter is asked again for someone just like you. And that may be a while.

The reason you received a "no"? It could be something as simple and tragic as the fact that you failed to speak of your very real accomplishments in terms that the organization values. It could be something as trivial as your personal style of dress. But if it's important enough to influence the search committee's decision to pursue or not to pursue, it's important enough to you and the recruiter. And so it's up to you to find out as much as you can in advance.

Have you ever noticed that the same names crop up again and again in the People in Business news columns announcing new hires for the top jobs? There is a reason why the same group of HR stars is routinely offered the plum opportunities that open up around the country. They are already known commodities. True, they're probably known on the conference circuits and they're probably the ones most routinely quoted in all the big business magazines, but they're also completely unambiguous about who they are in the HR world, what they stand for, and what they bring to the organizational culture. They can also unemotionally and strategically plot out their best career paths. They're even willing to turn down an opportunity if it doesn't completely fit their vision for the next step in their career. Moving up during the early years of their careers, they may not have been known to the world, but they're known to themselves. They know who they are, what they have to offer, and what they need at each next step of their own career paths. And they can speak fluently on the business issues that are the most compelling to the organization. And so the hiring committees have a clear picture of whom they are extending their opportunity to.

If it's a match, it's a *yes* from both sides. And it doesn't happen by accident; it happens after a lot of hard work and self-scrutiny all around. It's a buying and selling proposition in which both parties are really clear on what the product is and how valuable it is to both sides of the negotiation table. Consequently, *you* must be a known commodity, but first you have to know yourself. You have to be able to describe yourself, your experiences, and your skill sets clearly and comprehensively in terms that the hiring committee understands and can relate to. But first *you* have to know what your *product* is—you—and what you can offer eager and loyal customers—in this case your leadership teams, your employees, and the various selection committees you'll encounter throughout your career as you progress from opportunity to opportunity.

As you begin this book, you may be thinking to yourself that success is all about the résumé and who you know—what your education and experiences tell recruiters that you can do because you've already done them. It's not. It's about moving your product to market and being recognized. It's about being sought after. Sometimes it's about being associated with the right kinds of companies (for instance, one of *Fortune* magazine's Most Admired Companies). Or sometimes you're lucky enough to be associated with a lesser company and then you can tell the story of how you took on cultural and business challenges. Success is about how you make yourself be the best you can be so that the market will continue to want you, as opposed to someone else—and someone else's product. This means you must have all the components and features of your product organized, up-to-date, and ready to reconfigure and upgrade as the market trends demand.

CAREER KITTING

If you've ever purchased a computer from Dell, you're probably familiar with that mildly obsessive habit of tracking its custom assembly progress on-line. After the order is processed but before the computer can be assembled, your computer goes through a stage called *kitting*. All the necessary pieces and parts that go into successful computer manufacturing are assembled and placed in a "tote," which is like a big plastic tub, although the word calls to mind a canvas boater's bag sold by Lands' End or L.L. Bean. Keyboard, disk drives, motherboard, various memory cards, software, even the case: It all gets placed into the tote. And then the assembler has all he or she needs to put together a final product that you—the buying customer—can then put to use to meet your own objectives.

I'll return to the concept of career kitting throughout this book. For the moment, it's essential that we look at what is in your career kit currently and what additional elements you may need to add to it before you can build a world-class professional career product that is in demand. As you continue to build your product just the way you have thoughtfully designed it, you can then take yourself to the marketplace and present your product with the confidence that you have what it takes to add significant value to the HR operation. Why? Because along the way you have also assembled a community of potential customers who know what kind of professional you are, what features you offer, and how you can help them achieve their goals.

Let's look in your kit as it stands at the moment.

When client companies retain me to search for top HR executives, one of the most commonly requested attributes is *a successful track record showing progressively more skill and experience (responsibility and scope)*. In your career kit this translates into the knowledge, education, and experience that underlie everything else that you do and learn as a practicing professional. How far along in your formal education have you gone? What experiences did you have, even growing up, that have influenced the way you look at the world and process what you observe? Do you learn and produce quickly? Or slowly? Are you still upgrading your capabilities through frequent learning and experiential opportunities? Or does your résumé show evidence that you've stopped growing somewhere along the way?

My clients also ask for evidence of *business acumen*. Practical understanding of all the key issues faced by the other departments of your company—and how HR can serve those departments' needs—makes you an even more creative and effective business partner in your business. As you will read in the interviews of HR stars included in this book, several of the leaders at the top of their game look back at the time they dropped their MBA studies and regret it to this day. Seize every opportunity to add to your career kit experiences and training that will help you build this essential component of your product.

How are your *leadership skills*? Your product is about people, and hiring managers of A Player companies want to know that you bring with you the ability to lead, inspire, and motivate your company's employees throughout the organization. How well do you communicate with others? Can the people you work with communicate with you, knowing they're safe to share their opinions, insights, even bad news? Do you keep confidences well? Are you a compelling, persuasive speaker? Do you responsively take action on the input of others?

My client companies often ask for *breadth and depth of HR experience in at least two or three specialty areas, such as compensation, staffing, or organization development.* As you progress through the early years of your career, you would do well to build expertise in a few specialty areas, in addition to being conversant in HR from a generalist's role. Over time your expertise in these areas will help you sustain your personal credibility at times when your focused knowledge is more urgently needed than your more general perspectives. By the time you reach the pinnacle of your career and you are a serious candidate for the top opportunities in A Player companies, your expertise will give you the necessary *gravitas* and confidence to move forward toward the position of your career-long dreams.

Hiring managers also want to make sure you have already done in your previous roles what they are recruiting you to do in their companies. When I get the job order, this desire translates into *demonstrated ability to successfully deliver specific human resource services in a comparable company, industry, or work environment.* It's rare for a multi-billion-dollar company to seriously consider a candidate who ran an HR function in a $100-million to $500-million company, for example. Or if the hiring company has an international presence, you can be sure that company will only be interested in HR leaders who have not only done that but have been there, and there, and there, and there.

This ability gives you *credibility,* which is an additional feature my clients request. They want to know that you will be able to quickly gain the confidence of the other senior executives and board members, as well as the employees throughout the company. Can you assess situations, develop solutions, and present a clear, concise business case to support your recommendations?

As I was working on this chapter, the University of Michigan released its list of five key competencies for HR professionals, which has been endorsed by the Society for Human Resources Management (SHRM). I was not surprised to see that my list of six qualities most frequently asked for by clients is closely related to the University of Michigan's five competencies:

1. *Strategic contribution:* Can you elevate your perspective of day-to-day transaction activities and offer creative, big-picture plans that serve the company's long-term goals?
2. *Personal credibility:* In addition to your mastery of your profession and how it benefits company-wide objectives, do you command the respect and confidence of your colleagues? Do you have the reputation of being leaders in HR initiatives?
3. *HR delivery:* Do you have a track record of designing and delivering innovative HR programs that serve your company's objectives? Can you tell that story and back it up with a quantifiable narrative, assigning numerical value to your contributions?
4. *Business knowledge:* Do you understand how HR relates to the rest of the business in terms of your company's objectives? Can you talk about your people areas of concern using the vocabulary of the financial department? Research and development department? Legal? Production?
5. *HR technology:* Are you up-to-date on the various HR delivery programs, theories, products, practices, and, quite literally, technical innovations that support HR's delivery of essential services—especially those that will elevate you from that transactional role and open the doors for you to participate in higher-level strategic conversations?

There is nothing on either of these lists that is out of your reach. As you re-engineer your current product to serve your future market (a different employer, a different industry sector, different geographic region, or a larger company), simply consider the components you have in your current career kit. If you notice that there's a missing piece, make sure your next move will give you the chance to add that piece to your metaphorical tote. In this way, you are always modifying or redesigning your product to achieve your goals as they transform over the years (which they will as you become more confident and ambitious yourself).

When you look at your career simply as a product, you can more effectively consider its strengths and weaknesses in the context of the customers you want to sell that product to. Only you can define for yourself what HR career success looks like. And then you must masterfully engineer the many pieces of your assembly that will make your product the best purchase decision to be made by the employer of *your* choice for the leadership-bound position of strength of *your* making.

WHY MONEY GETS LEFT ON THE TABLE

As this book is being written, we are in a down economy. In a few short years we have swung 180 degrees from being in a "War for Talent," where employers were desperate to fill seats, to being a nation where most people will agree that "there's nobody out there hiring." But that's not true. Whether we're in a good economy or a bad one, one fact remains essentially the same: *There are always fabulous jobs that need to be filled.* In fact, the jobs that are open today are even better than they were during the so-called boom years. Employers must be more mindful of getting the absolute most and best out of every new hire. They have fewer slots they can fill; therefore employers must pack into that opportunity as much value to the ideal candidate as possible. Consequently, while there may be fewer jobs available, those that are open represent fantastic opportunities for ambitious HR careerists.

And that's not going to change when the economy improves again. With each cycle of economic robustness, we learn that much more about how to attract and apply talent to organizational objectives. No matter what the economy is doing, the *really* smart employers recognize that passion and professionalism throughout the ranks are always essential and valued ingredients for corporate vitality and viability. So employees who know how to express and demonstrate their passion for excellence will always be in demand. The jobs may be fewer, but those that exist are by necessity more substantial. There is more opportunity to learn, engage your skills, and have an impact on the organization overall (even on your community). Each job must count for more than it used to. Therefore, you must be able to *account* for more than you used to—and be able to discuss your HR accomplishments in a vocabulary that everyone throughout the corporate leadership ranks can identify with and value.

And the lessons we're learning now will still be valid as the economy swings toward abundance again. This is the time for HR to shine, and those who will be successful in the long term are those who are paying the closest attention right now. Those will be the true HR business leaders we keep hearing about in the HR press. In good times and in bad, the HR career message is still the same: Be discerning. Have a plan. Recognize and take advantage of great opportunities when they unfold before you. Likewise, be willing to turn your back on fabulous offers that just aren't right for you.

It's hard to turn your back on attractive jobs, especially for the opportunity for a change in environment or more money when such chances aren't coming as frequently as they used to. But this is one of the main reasons why recruiters watch money being left on the table—*the assumption that there just aren't enough jobs out there.* By grabbing the first opportunity that comes your way, you could be reaching for false gold. Perhaps the next one would have been even more promising, with both better compensation and greater opportunity to learn and grow inside an organization that truly values human resources. But you can't take it because you're already freshly committed.

Or you lack knowledge and/or experience in the opportunity before you. Perhaps your knowledge and experience are inappropriate for the region or industry you want to work in. Is your area heavily unionized and you have no experience in labor law? Get some classes under your belt, at least. Be willing to take a demotion, if you must, to expose yourself to real-life labor relations experience. If you want to live eventually in Northern California, would it be helpful to have experience in a high-tech company? Certainly. If you don't have it already, seek out high-tech experience where you live now and strategize your way toward building a solid high-tech-oriented résumé (and the personal contacts that go with the experience) that will eventually be your ticket to Silicon Valley. Do you want to live in Miami, or Boston, or Washington, DC, or Cheyenne, or Phoenix? The first thing to do is research the workplace issues your desired location is facing—make sure you have some credibility, some value to offer in those areas. No matter what the change is, if you don't have the firsthand experience, make sure you have some current knowledge on the subject so that you can at least speak fluently about it. More importantly, demonstrate that you have a healthy and informed respect for the differences and that you have given thoughtful consideration as to how you would approach working in the new environment.

The last thing you want to do is sound presumptuous. For example, I recall one discussion in particular with a staffing director in a non-technology company in Connecticut. The candidate had very good staffing experience but was clueless about what the differences might be in recruiting engineers in the heart of Silicon Valley (where the position was located) during the dot.com boom. When asked about how he would address the competitive issues associated with staffing at the time, he said, "We have a competitive market in Connecticut. It can't be much different." Wrong. I can guarantee you they did not have thousands of companies competing for a single candidate located within a twenty-five-mile radius nor candidates with five offers in hand shopping for a sixth one. He should have done his homework.

Or you have the experience but you forgot to say so. Recruiters do their best to match background with the requests specified by the search committees. But it's up to you to make sure the interviewers believe that you can provide what they're looking for. Only you can sell it. Too many times candidates will discover after the fact that the hiring committee wasn't convinced they had the experience they need to take the company to the next phase of its objectives, even though the candidates had exactly that experience in a previous company. Didn't they understand that you had this, this, and this experience that's right up their alley? No, they didn't understand. And the recruiter isn't likely to go back and straighten them out. Everyone's on to the next candidate for consideration.

You lack positioning and negotiating skills that would keep you in that position of strength. You're either too anxious or not anxious enough, and you send the search committee the wrong message about your passion and interest in the position. If you appear over-eager, the committee might say, "That person wants the job a little too badly. There must be something wrong here." Or if you play it cool and dignified (at least your version of cool and dignified), the committee might read that signal as aloof or disinterested. There are many ways you can express interest and passion in the company without coming across as desperate. We'll get into those ways later in this book.

Or you're clueless about the buzz. Do you know what the community is saying about you? Your company? The HR department itself? You need that information, even if it's bad. Then you can tackle that problem head-on within the context of the interview. Sometimes the HR department—or the HR leader personally—must play the "heavy" during a certain situation or initiative. Word gets out, without benefit of understanding the surrounding circumstances. If you know what that word is, you can control the direction of that particular aspect of the interview and turn it to your advantage.

Or you leave money on the table because you simply don't ask for it. HR candidates who are clueless about their value to their target marketplace may be so eager for the new opportunity that they're afraid to negotiate for a more valuable package for themselves. That's understandable. We're all human and we let our fears and emotions govern our actions during the most critical moment in discussions. However, keep in mind that effective negotiating results not only in more money off the table and into your pocket, but also in an elevated respect for the kind of businessperson you are. Search committees want to know that you can do business on your own behalf. That's the best assurance that you will be able to do business on the company's behalf as well.

Table 1.1 shows the broad range of income potential that you can realize as you progress through your years in HR. This is just a *taste* of what

Table 1.1. Virtually Unlimited Earning Potential.

Position	*Range of Pay*	*Sample Titles*
Entry Level	$30,000-$50,000	Human Resources Generalist I
		Benefits Analyst I
		Compensation Analyst I
		Employee Relations Representative I
		Labor Relations Representative I
		Recruiter
		Training Specialist I
Intermediate Level	$50,000-$60,000	Human Resources Generalist II
		Benefits Analyst II
		Compensation Analyst II
		EEO/Diversity Specialist
		Employee Relations Representative II
		HRIS Specialist
		Labor Relations Representative II
		Organization Development Specialist
		Pension Plan Administrator
		Recruiter
		Training Specialist II
Career/Senior Level	$60,000-$75,000	Human Resources Generalist III
		Benefits Administrator
		Compensation Administrator
		Compensation Analyst III
		Senior Recruiter (IT)
		Senior Recruiter (Management)
		Training Specialist III

Table 1.1. Virtually Unlimited Earning Potential, Cont'd.

Position	*Range of Pay*	*Sample Titles*
Manager Level	$75,000-$100,000	Human Resources Manager
		Benefits Manager
		Compensation Manager
		EEO/Diversity Manager
		Employee Assistance Program Manager
		Employee Relations Manager
		Employment Manager
		HRIS Manager
		Human Resources Call Center Manager
		Labor Relations Manager
		Management Development Manager
		Organization Development Manager
		Pension Planning and Administration Manager
		Safety Manager
		Training Manager
		Worklife Manager
Director Level	$100,000-$135,000	Human Resources Director
		Benefits Director
		Compensation and Benefits Director
		Compensation Director
		EEO/Diversity Director
		Employment Director
		Training Director
Executive/VP Level	$130,000-$190,000	Top Labor Relations Executive
		Top Compensation and Benefits Executive
		Top Compensation Executive
		Top Executive Compensation Executive
		Top Benefits Executive
		Top Employment Executive
		Top Training and Development Executive
		Top Human Resources Planning Executive
		Top EEO/Diversity Executive
		Top Human Resources Operations Executive

Table 1.1. Virtually Unlimited Earning Potential, Cont'd.

Position	*Range of Pay*	*Sample Titles*
		Top Human Resources Shared Services Executive
Top HR Executive	$225,000-$375,000	Top Human Resources Executive

**All data are effective 3/1/2003, from Towers Perrin surveys. Data reflects salary ranges on a national basis; used with permission.*

is to come in your future. Improvements in the economy, the success and growth of your company, the ways you might eventually leverage your experience into consulting or paid speaking engagements, can all serve to increase your own personal income potential. It's really up to you.

THERE ARE MANY PATHS TO THE TOP

As we've said before, HR as a profession is still discovering the many paths to career success. While it's by no means the new kid on the corporate block, it's very much a late bloomer—only now after many decades coming into and claiming its own power to be a significant contributor to corporate objectives and initiatives. And so it follows that the leadership-bound career path has not yet been completely defined and paved over for smooth (but limited) passage. There are many ways to the top, still, but they can be muddy and slippery and rife with false starts and dead ends.

But you can get started anywhere. You can be a Fulbright scholar. You could have done a stint at the London School of Economics. You could have an MBA from Harvard. Or an associate's certificate at any number of local community colleges. Or, like Jim Wall, Deloitte & Touche's national managing director of HR, you could have been a trailing spouse scanning the Help Wanteds in your new city's newspaper, looking for a new way to use the skills and experiences you gained in your old job. It doesn't matter how or where you put your foot on the HR career path. But it does matter how you take the next steps, and then the next.

And it matters how you regard the overall kitting of your career and your assembled knowledge and experiences. And then it matters how you can tell the story, which we will talk about in the next chapter.

That is how you will develop your position of strength. That is what's going to differentiate you from your competitors for the next great opportunity that's making its way to you even now.

And *that* is what we're going to help you learn how to achieve.

How to Break In

There are many paths to the top in HR. There are also many doors into the profession itself. Although more and more people are entering HR after specifically studying for it in college, there are still plenty of ways to transition into HR from other corporate functions. No matter where you are in the company, HR can also use your expertise. The experience you have gained in other areas may have provided you skills (often referred to as *transferable* skills) that could help you easily transition into an HR role. For example:

Function	*Transferable Skills*	*Could Transition to*
Accounting	Math, data analysis, detail-orientation	Compensation or Benefits
Sales	Ability to assess needs and influence people	Recruiting
Marketing Communications	Writing and presentation skills	Employee Communications
Legal	Employment law, contract law, negotiating resolutions	Employee Relations or Compliance
Information Technology (IT)	Programming, report writing, systems and software technology	Human Resources Information Technology (HRIT)
Administrative	Scheduling, coordinating meetings, data entry, writing and phone skills	HR Administration, Benefits Administration, or Recruitment Coordination (which could lead to HR Representative or Generalist roles with additional training and experience)

SUMMARY

Success in HR is within your reach, as long as you strategically manage your career choices over time:

- As you lay out your career plan, think in terms of career kitting, in which you assemble the necessary skills and experiences to qualify for your ultimate career goals.
- Think of your combined package of skills and experiences as a product to move to the marketplace.
- No matter what the economy is doing, there are always fabulous jobs that need to be filled.
- There are many paths to the top. This book will help you identify the routes that will ensure your success!

INTERVIEW

Paul Bianchi

Senior Vice President, Human Resources, PeopleSoft, Inc.

AS THE TOP HR EXECUTIVE for PeopleSoft, Paul Bianchi heads the people function of one of the most prominent HR suppliers in the world. The second-largest enterprise application software provider, PeopleSoft employs thirteen thousand workers in 150 countries.

Entering the profession over fifteen years ago, Paul immediately saw opportunities to elevate the HR function to one that would command greater respect and stature at the senior-most levels of the organization. In this interview he discusses the essential qualities HR professionals must have to develop themselves throughout their careers and achieve that kind of influence and impact when the company's most important strategic decisions are made.

What was the best piece of advice you have ever received?

Actually it was a piece of advice [a former boss had given me] that was completely wrong. But it was valuable to me because it forced me to continue thinking about it as I've progressed through my career. He told me that the best HR work is transparent. That's completely wrong. If you're not clearly adding and contributing to the business proposition of the company, you quickly create questions about whether or not you should be in that job—or if the company should have that position at all. Of course, you have to balance that with the need to not appear overly concerned with politicizing your contributions or marketing your image too aggressively. Still, overall, one of the things that HR professionals probably have not done as well as other professions and functions is say, "Here's how we're going to contribute to the bottom line, here's our goal, here's how we're doing against it, here's how we're making ourselves part of creating value for our shareholders."

How do you achieve that level of exposure and branding and stay within the boundaries of acceptable behavior, especially when the HR professional may be uncomfortable with that kind of scrutiny?

To be an effective HR leader in a company of any significant size, you have to be prepared to be in the white light. HR people have been too willing to retreat into the back office, saying, "We support the business; we make management run well." I don't think there's anything wrong with that emphasis, per se, but I do think it undermines the contributions that are more tangible, even if they're still qualitative and harder to measure in real numbers. You apply the human capital disciplines to the business needs, and in some cases that requires counterintuitive HR behaviors. Overall in HR, there's not enough accountability. We're not seeing the kind of performance we need, and we're not holding HR professionals accountable for driving performance consistently upward.

Are you suggesting such changes as having HR professionals alter their vocabulary and find other ways to insinuate themselves into circles of other business partners they might not have otherwise?

"Insinuate" is a good word. Make it important for business leaders to pay attention to the human capital side. It's about language. It's about relationships. It's about proving worth. And that's where the clarity of human capital needs to come to the forefront. That's how you move out of the back office into the front office.

What was the moment your career changed forever?

I got a "battlefield" promotion when my boss left the company and other senior people followed shortly thereafter. I quickly needed to figure out how to make contributions above simply functional expertise. I needed to learn to assert myself as a member of the management team and address issues they thought were most important, as well as the ones I thought were most important. It thrust me into a sink-or-swim role and changed my perception of what kind of impact I could have, even at a super-peer level.

What is the one thing you wish you had done differently?

I wish I had started my career in a bigger company. While I had the opportunity to do different things in a smaller company, I didn't get the kind of good base foundation that I think would have benefited me even more.

What is the best piece of advice you have to offer new HR professionals?

You have to take a very aggressive responsibility toward your own development. HR professionals who differentiate themselves are the ones who are not content with learning only what their company has to teach them. They're out making connections, going to HR workshops, joining professional associations.

They're also the ones who have sought out mentoring relationships, even with senior people outside of HR. Learn from mentors in other parts of the business what makes those kinds of people successful. Go figure out what it takes to be a great salesperson in your company. Have the courage to say, "Hey, Mr. Vice President, can I buy you a cup of coffee? I'd really like to learn more about how you got to the position you're in and what that means for young people like me." You have to have the courage to step up and ask for time.

What is the best thing that new entrants into the profession can do for themselves?

I encourage people everywhere to pop their heads up every 1.5 to 2 years to figure out whether they are doing what they really want to do, are in the right place, with the right kind of people and the right kind of company. Without that constant opportunity in front of you to do new things, learn new things, be involved in different dynamics, and expand your opportunities, you will lose your passion for the profession, and your commitment to excellence and growth will disintegrate rapidly.

What is the worst thing they can do?

Stay in their office and think that doing email is work. One thing I've told my generalists as they come in is, "If you don't have to buy a pair of shoes every six to eight months, you're not doing your job."

What do you think about the bad reputation that HR professionals tend to suffer, such as being slaves to "administrivia" and not getting the respect they deserve?

I think you make your own reality. If you allow yourself to buy into that reputation, you'll never have the courage to break out and figure out how HR can become a vital part of the business. It's an ongoing battle, no question about it. If you're not aggressive about your pursuit in connecting human capital discipline with business results, then you will be consigned to the fate that you create for yourself.

INTERVIEW

Susan Bowick

Executive Vice President, Human Resources and Workforce Development, Hewlett-Packard Corporation

IN 1977, SUSAN BOWICK was a dissatisfied Colorado teacher just coming to realize that she despaired at the thought of pursuing that profession for the rest of her life. At the offhand suggestion of her husband, she casually applied for a job as a secretary at Hewlett-Packard. Her interviewer, however, spotted higher qualifications and offered her a job as a business analyst. She moved into HR two years later and invested her entire career in growing the people side of the business.

The project that tops her HR career was the controversial merger of Hewlett-Packard (HP) and Compaq—two distinctly separate cultures that, combined, would expand her employee base from 86,000 to almost 150,000 literally overnight. In this interview, conducted just before her retirement announcement, she talks about the major lessons of her career and how she grew along the way.

What is the best piece of advice you ever received?

When I was a little girl, my German grandmother had a saying: "Remember the sun doesn't shine every day." When everything doesn't go well, that's normal. As I got older I had a lot of opportunities to remind myself: "Well, this was a learning experience; this wasn't a good day, but I won't let it throw me off course." This advice was a very big part of the foundation of who I am. I expect things to go up and down and not always be perfect. I've always believed that you can figure out a way through even the most difficult mistake or conflict-ridden mess.

I actually have shared it with others over the years when I can tell someone has been thrown by heavy workload or something he or she didn't expect and it's affecting his or her attitude. The person hasn't developed the coping skills to go through the down times.

What was the moment that changed your career forever?

It was when I decided to get out of teaching and start at HP. I was teaching business subjects at the high school and community college level, and I was miserable. I woke up one day and said, "I just can't imagine myself doing this for the next twenty to thirty years." My husband, who had run a junior achievement program for HP, had seen an ad for a glorified secretarial job for the company. He said, "Susan, I think you have the personality to fit in there, and you'd really like HP. Why don't you send in your résumé?"

I said, "Oh, I've got my degree. I worked as a secretary to get through college. I don't want to go back and do that!" He said, "Just give it a try."

Once I got over my original objections, I sent in my résumé. I had to go down and take them work samples—which was demeaning to me because I was *teaching* those subjects! The boss who interviewed me for the job offered me a job more as a business analyst rather than strict secretarial work, and my life really changed. I started doing something where I wasn't confined by a job description or rigid structure, like teaching had been. I was able to use my creativity, figuring out what needed to be done. I had found a place where I could think.

The other step "back" was inside HP when the man I worked for got a promotion. By that time I was in a group HR manager job, which was pretty high in HP. There were two of us in that position at that point, and I knew my boss didn't need two group HR managers. But he didn't make the move to say whether it would be me or this other guy. So I was the one who decided, "This is for the birds."

I saw a job that was open inside HP. It wasn't in the Bay Area. It was in San Diego and several levels lower than I was. It was a site personnel manager, but it was in a business I had never worked in. I had been a site personnel manager before. I knew that I liked it. So I volunteered to be interviewed, and I took the transfer to San Diego. Again, it was a demotion. My colleagues thought I was nuts. It wasn't the traditional onward and upward career path. But I did it so I could go learn and experience a different part of the business I didn't know.

How did that benefit you in the long term?

Ultimately, I think that move is what got me here today. It was a move into the printer business. I went from site personnel manager to group personnel manager over all of HP's printer business in less than a year. And then my boss at the time was promoted to having 80 percent of HP's business, and I went with him to where I then had 80 percent of the global HR business at HP. When Pete Peterson, my predecessor, retired, he had identified two of us as internal candidates who were most likely to be considered for his replacement. I was the one, luckily, who was selected for the corporate job.

Not only did you have a track record of doing good work throughout your career, you also had the good fortune of being noticed. Do you have any suggestions on how HR professionals can make sure their contributions actually get the attention of the people who can help them along in their careers?

I try to look at the world through my boss's eyes, not just mine. I've always found in HR, in particular, if you understand the business, the organization structure, the culture, HR is just a candy store of tools to help the boss get better results through people. And so bosses don't look at it as "HR for HR's sake." They start seeing it as a marvelous contribution. And it's worked time after time after time that the boss in the organization got better results than he would have on his own.

It's because I have always felt my priority has been to make the business more competitive and to make it a better place to work from the employees' standpoint. These two objectives don't have to be at odds with each other. Let's face it. A lot of the things we deal with are the things the line managers are the least comfortable with. Many of the line teams appreciate someone who helps them be better at parts of the job that they might naturally avoid.

What would you have done differently if you could do it over again?

I wish I had worked overseas earlier in my career. I didn't realize how important globalization is and the need to understand from firsthand experience different cultures and different ways of viewing what is a U.S.-centric company. For a variety of reasons

I didn't actively go after that when it was brought up earlier in my career. And, knowing what I know now, I would have.

A lot of the emerging markets and untapped skill sets are in Asia, Eastern Europe, Middle East, Russia. Get ahead of it today. Those are the places I would take a transfer to—and learn as much as I could about the regional expansion firsthand.

What advice do you have to share with HR professionals on their way up?

Don't think that the only way to progress is up. Be really willing to actively pursue horizontal moves, even demotions, if you're going to learn something that's new, that's going to be vital, that's going to help you understand a part of the company or a part of the HR skill set that you don't currently have.

As long as you're learning and building your skill sets, don't pay that much attention to job title or pay levels—the short-term rewards. Careers are a long-term thing. And I see a lot of people limiting their thinking by only looking at a vertical progression.

What do HR professionals need now that you didn't need when you started your career?

The first thing that comes to my mind is that you have to bring into HR some of the same technology and practices it takes to run the business. Knowing what it takes to go fast, to enable basic things, is just entry into the game today. It's not the complete job. Ten or fifteen years ago, if you were able to run a huge global project, that was a breakthrough. Today, we in HR have had to *lead* the use of technology to enable integration. Build on that and do things like knowledge management, metrics, and global workforce surveys.

The second thing, which I mentioned earlier, is the ability to work globally. Frequently, our most effective teams are dispersed global teams that have figured out how to work together. Technology again is an enabler. All of a sudden you can select the best talent anywhere in the world, no matter where they sit, bring them together, and get them productive. This is an example of how technology and the ability to operate globally enables a company in a way that hasn't been done before.

What is the best thing new entrants can do for themselves?

You need to understand the business you're working in first, and you do have to speak the language of the business. Part of what has held HR back, as compared to IT and Finance, for instance, is that frequently we can speak the language of HR first but cannot clearly articulate how it benefits the business. Or we're not comfortable with talking in business terms. If you use the vast capabilities and resources in HR and position them in terms of what they will do to help the business become more successful, or a better place for the employees to work, you get much better results and a much better connection with line teams who ultimately have to jointly own everything that HR brings to the table. And so, to me, that is the most critical foundational skill for the HR professional.

I think every new entrant should have some accounting classes, some business law classes, and some economics classes. I don't think you have to have an MBA, but you should go to an executive program and be familiar with case study methodology.

How important is it for the HR practitioner to actually have a passion for the company's product?

I don't think that one is a make-or-break issue. My first twelve years were in test and measurement, and I never fell in love with the dynamic signal analyzer. I just felt happy if I could describe what our customers did with it. You have to have an appreciation for what it takes to develop and design and sell the product.

There are other businesses, like the businesses that HP is in now, that you *can* get passionate about: digital imaging, printers, PCs, and more consumer products. I don't think it's a prerequisite that you love the project or be passionate about what you're producing. But you need to understand it. Understand the whole product life cycle. You need to understand the development, manufacture, distribution, service, where the money is made, and the interdependence and connections among all those things. You need to understand that whole profit model, product inception, on through customer use and disposal.

What's the worst thing HR professionals can do to limit their potential?

In general, if someone looks for approval or direction from others before taking a risk, regardless of what you set out to do, you're going to be limited by other people's opinions of where you come from. It can be especially true in HR, where a lot of people don't expect very much from you. Starting out, if I lived up only to those expectations—or *down* to those expectations, I should say—it would have been a very disappointing career. Line managers need the HR team to set high expectations, articulate them, and then deliver.

What characteristics and qualities do you look for when hiring a new HR professional?

It's hard not to have ten pages of everything that can go into this profession. But there are certainly a set of core characteristics that make up the foundation.

You need to be *value-oriented.* You need to have an internal focus of control. You're going to have to deal with a lot of conflict and change and situations where there is no cookbook. So you have to be very well grounded, have a sense of humor and objectivity, and not be seen as a political player. And you need to be able to go to sleep at night and get up the next day with the personal stamina and objectivity to be able to help the organization. You need to have a strong personal base.

And, of course, you have to have a *business orientation.* You have to be able to speak the language of line management, profit and loss, and synthesize out HR implications of what the business or management team needs.

We all need some *technical competence*: labor law, the ability to deliver training programs, and the ability to work across functions. We tend to operate in silos inside the HR department, which doesn't help our customers. Our line managers want an integrated service from HR. They don't want to get a set of salary ranges here, a set of evaluation processes here, the annual stock program here. They want someone to present this to them in terms of an integrated performance *system.* In order to do that, HR people have to work across functional silos. I don't expect people to be *experts* across the silos, but I expect them to understand where there is a place for them to connect what they're doing with everyone else. And to be able to lead a team of other specialists who may not be in their area of expertise, and be more solution-oriented and not be a stand-alone producer.

That's why HR sometimes gets a bad rap. They forget to look at what they do from the manager's perspective.

When did you take a risk in your career and have it pay off?

Not to be melodramatic, but every day you have to take risks, intervene, and bring issues to the table that other people might just as soon ignore. The real risk is when you don't deal with the conflict.

We call it "moose launching." Blast that thing right into the middle of the table! It means frequently I have to be the person who gets that issue that everyone is talking about around the cooler onto the table and make it a legitimate topic of discussion. I have this iceberg model that shows how typically all line managers gravitate to what we see above the waterline. It's all that happens *below* the waterline—how power is distributed, how we deal with conflict, how we deal with protracted periods of uncertainty where people don't know what tomorrow may bring—that is where the real issues lie. Actively managing that—I think that's a daily act of risk taking for a lot of HR professionals.

You're the one who has to understand the dynamics below the waterline and get those issues on the table. If you don't work them through, along with the hard issues, you'll never get the results you need.

So what's the pain you feel when you launch the moose?

It's usually the question: Am I the only one who thinks we should work on this? If I launch the moose, is there going to be anyone else in the room who will also say, "Yes, that's an issue." No matter how experienced you are, other people are going to look at you like, "Man, are you ever coming in from left field!"

With experience, you learn how to trust your judgment and sixth sense.

Have you ever thought about doing anything other than HR?

Not once I got in it. I just found it to be the most complex and challenging and rewarding thing that I could possibly do.

2

EVERY CHOICE TELLS A STORY

In this chapter you will discover how a lifetime of career choices can lead you in the direction of your long-term ambitions. As you track your choices, you must also put them in a context of meaningful accomplishments.

I HAD BEEN LOOKING forward to meeting Anita for several days. Her résumé couldn't have been better—respectably long stints at well-regarded A Player companies. On paper she was a perfect candidate for a specific search I was conducting. She came highly recommended by people whose judgment I respect and trust. And when she walked in the door she was polished to perfection—not too overdressed for this casual environment. Yet not too under-dressed either (which is a very fine line to walk when you're an executive in Silicon Valley). The impression she gave, based on both her appearance and résumé, was that she was definitely on the fast track to a senior executive position before too long, if she wasn't there already.

But then she opened her mouth. And the illusion dissipated like fairy dust. She just didn't have anything to say. She couldn't formulate a cogent, succinct answer to any of my questions. She couldn't organize the substance of my questions into any meaningful context, and so out came long, wandering speeches that amounted to gobble-de-gook. After a few futile attempts to coach her, I wound up the meeting as quickly as I could and still be polite. After seeing her off at the door—she still hadn't stopped talking—I disappointedly set her résumé aside. There was no way I could present her to my client company. If she was unable to articulate what she had done to me with encouragement and patience, what would my client think?

It was too bad and a real disappointment. But on reflection, I realized that it shouldn't be surprising that many HR professionals—even the successful ones—can't organize their experience and credentials into a meaningful framework that will help them track their career step by step toward their own chosen ultimate ambition. The current iteration of HR as a profession came of age in the 1970s and 1980s when we were still struggling in the confusing employer's world of "Just Be Glad You Have a Job." The HR function was more of a staff role at that time, with an administrative bent, rather than a business function able to contribute to corporate objectives. True, there were many, many very successful corporate senior vice presidents of HR (many of whom cycled through that assignment as part of their regular corporate rotation; five years later you could just as easily find them in marketing). And true, there were also many, many career HR professionals who felt deep in their bones that they were somehow called to the profession, and had been in HR (or *personnel*) their entire careers.

But actual, *planned* success in HR? Well, as with almost every other profession in those days, it was more often than not a matter of sheer luck. Until recently not much has been done to identify exactly what it takes to maximize your full potential in HR. Although the recent release of the five basic competencies by the University of Michigan has given us a picture of the basic buckets of skills a truly arrived HR professional must have, we still didn't have a sense of exactly what the steps were to accomplish those competencies and use them to rise intentionally through the organizational levels of a company. So no wonder Anita had difficulties organizing her answers to my questions in the context that would be relevant to her accomplishments as discrete examples of her abilities; as indications of how she can help any organization arrive at potent HR solutions; or as components of her overall career trajectory.

In other words, she lacked *context*—as do most HR careerists who pursue opportunities for success and growth without any real big-picture view of how each decision, each move, could influence their careers in the long term. Again, the fundamental principle of this book is that you have more control over your career than you think you do! And to make full use of that control, and have it lead you where you want to go, it's essential that you have something of a roadmap of the various avenues and options within the HR profession. You may have seen similar diagrams before in other books, but they are usually in the context of the organization and its needs. In this chapter we'll be talking about how HR breaks down into its many components from the standpoint of *your* career and *your* needs and ambitions.

What Anita lacked is the same thing that many HR professionals lack—the ability to tell her story. With the bird's-eye perspective of the overall career landscape that this chapter offers, you will be able to tell your own story, in all its many contexts, so that you can cogently frame your credentials and contributions in such a way that you're paving the road ahead of you before you even get there.

LIFE IS LONG; YOUR OPTIONS ARE MANY

Each choice you make in your career leads you toward your future. And while there are very few missteps you can't recover from, a carefully plotted approach to your career and working life in three- to five-year increments will help you string together a story of accomplishment and progressive growth that will captivate hiring managers and search committees for years to come.

You can decide how that story is told and at what pace. You can take the direct, fast route to your ultimate goals (absorbing some loss in terms of family life and non-work-related passions and interests). Or you can take the "scenic route," stopping along the way to thoroughly enjoy the scenery. Or you can do both. The choice is yours. The only assumption I am making in this book is that you are *leadership-bound.*

And you have plenty of time to get there. Careers can last a lifetime these days. People are retiring later in life, out of choice, not just from necessity. And more and more people have more than one career during their lifetimes. Recent government statistics tell us that men live an average of 75.5 years, women 79.5 years. If you graduate college at age twenty-two, you are very likely to be in the job market for thirty, maybe even forty years. The fast track is great, but it is not for everyone. Make life and career decisions that make sense for you. And take comfort in knowing that you can always adjust your direction as you go along.

YOUR THREE BASIC HR CAREER CHOICES

Let's get started in dissecting the many elements that make up every HR career. There are three most fundamental components: Specialist, Generalist, and Executive. They are what I call the primary HR career paths. Each one is distinct from the other, but you can jump back and forth among the paths as you progress in your career.

Specialists are experts in a specific area within the human resource function; for instance, organization development, training, compensation, benefits, HRIT (human resources information technology), employee relations, labor relations, or staffing.

Generalists have a working knowledge (but not necessarily *in-depth* knowledge) of a variety of HR functions I listed above. They are typically assigned to a client group, which may consist of a line function such as marketing, sales, product development, manufacturing, finance, or administration. Generalists might also be assigned to a business unit in a large company. (Business units often consist of product development and marketing functions for a specific product group.) The business unit typically relies on centralized corporate functions for delivery of HR services. But it looks to its resident generalists for more custom support, designed specifically to fit the needs of that particular part of the organization.

Generalists typically provide a broad range of advisory or consulting services to the client group they are assigned to with regard to human capital management. Titles for individuals in HR generalist roles vary: HR generalist, HR consultant, HR business partner, HR manager, and even HR director. In small companies (fewer than 1,000 employees), the top HR job (which may carry the title of Vice President, Director, or Chief People Officer) may be a generalist role. In these situations, specialist functions, such as compensation plan design and benefits administration, are often farmed out to outsourcing firms or external consultants. These specialist roles typically report to the vice president of human resources in larger companies.

In an *executive* role, you could be the head of a specialty function or the top executive in the HR function, usually the vice president (or senior vice president or executive vice president) of human resources. You might also be called Chief People Officer. You could be the vice president or director of a function such as organization development (OD), staffing, compensation, or any number of other specialty areas. Or you could be the vice president or director responsible for the delivery of human resource services to the line. In any case, the executive role is a topmost function carrying with it a strong expectation for a strategic advisory role for the other executives.

Confusion begins among these three paths when people misinterpret the *generalist* title as a low-level HR administrative or even HR representative position. It's common for entry-level HR professionals to find themselves in introductory roles, which is appropriate, especially when they are in a large organization with a strong development tradition. It's like taking survey courses in college, a smattering of this and a smattering of that. These roles may very often carry the title of "HR Generalist"; but for the purposes of this book, they should not be confused with senior-level business partner roles, which I define as generalists.

However, it's also appropriate that the senior HR executive in the company is fundamentally a generalist. While that person doesn't have to be an expert in all functions associated with HR, he or she should at least be conversant in those areas and know exactly whom to turn to for more specialist-level expertise. In addition, if there is a senior HR executive on executive committees or boards, that person serves as the generalist supporting that group. So without a doubt, the generalist path is absolutely a high-potential freeway to the C-suite (the chief HR officer at the executive table).

Conversely, the specialist role may carry with it the impression of high-level prestige, but if you spend your entire career knee-deep in, say, compensation, you may be limiting your qualifications for the top executive spots. That alone may not necessarily be a bad thing, though. Maybe you love compensation and are really pretty lukewarm about staffing. Fair enough. Stay on that specialty trajectory and achieve the highest-most executive positions serving exclusively that function. And then, if you still feel as though you want to go further but can't within the corporate organization, jump off the corporate track altogether and become a consultant—eventually making even more money than the senior vice presidents who are your clients.

Pick one path or pick all three and move back and forth among them. Again the choice is yours. Just be sure you can discuss those choices coherently as business decisions when recruiters and search committees ask you for the logic behind your résumé.

•

Why Do Non-HR Professionals Get the Top People Seat?

It's a fact of the profession that the road to the senior vice president of HR spot is not straight and sure. It's probably the one chief executive position at "the table" that has many points of entry and opportunities for non-HR professionals to be successful. This is understandably frustrating for dedicated HR careerists who have followed their carefully designed and scheduled plan to the top, only to discover that their first likely opportunity was snapped up by someone who doesn't know a thing about HR.

Over the years I've watched many non-HR professionals get the coveted top spot, and here is a list of the most common reasons why:

- The new people chief is the CEO's best friend, someone who "can do anything."
- The outgoing people chief was so incompetent or unpopular that he or she instilled deep distrust or disrespect of HR throughout the entire culture. So the CEO or search committee recruits a known entity—someone who is highly regarded for his or her personal values and intelligence.
- Top management doesn't understand the full scope of what HR can do and needs to know in order to be effective.

If you are passed over for the top spot in favor of a non-HR professional, that is understandably a bitter pill to swallow. But it could be an excellent opportunity to influence the direction of HR in your company's immediate future. That person is going to need a trusted HR expert. You may be able to drive much of the HR initiative behind the scenes, change the company's regard for what HR can really do, and gather much-needed senior leadership experience that you can then package and market elsewhere to a new company.

•

EDUCATION

One of my favorite success principles is as follows:

Preparation + Opportunity = Success

We'll discuss the opportunity part of the equation throughout the rest of the book. This chapter is dedicated to the way you prepare yourself to be qualified to grasp those opportunities as they come along. And the first component of preparation is, of course, what kind of advantages you give yourself through education.

HR continues to be an emerging profession. No matter how long its function has been present inside an organization, there is still a tremendous amount of disagreement as to what kind of educational background makes HR candidates the most competitive. What I hear most often from clients is that they expect a minimum of a bachelor's degree for HR professionals and prefer a master's (the number-one specification requested by my clients is an MBA because of the emphasis on business). In taking a quick look at *Fortune*'s list of 100 Best Companies to Work For (which is only one indicator of HR success), I found that, of the sixty-two public companies that made the list, forty-six listed their HR vice presidents on their "Key People" listing on the on-line industry information site, Hoovers.com. Of those, only eighteen provided bios. Of the eighteen, the top degrees held by incumbents broke down as follows:

- Bachelor's only 8
- Master's 3
- MBA 4
- Ph.D. 2
- JD 1

Of the thirty-eight private companies that made the list, twenty-three provided names and titles of their top HR professional on the Key People listing—six listed HR directors, one had an HR coordinator, and sixteen had vice presidents of HR. Only two provided bios, and both of those had a bachelor's listed as the top degree held.

Although this is a minimal sample size, I believe it does reveal a bit about the educational background top companies expect when hiring senior HR professionals.

While an MBA may not be absolutely necessary in performing the HR functions, HR stars agree that it gives them a native fluency in overall business perspective and processes and vocabulary that gives them both confidence and credibility when they are working with their non-HR colleagues.

So to conclude: Don't let your basic education stop you from achieving the objectives you are aiming for. There are still companies that value firsthand experience over book learning. But those companies will become fewer and fewer as the years go by. Expect increasing pressure for you to gain broader business education and credibility the higher up the organization chart you want to rise. And many of those current senior vice presidents who don't have MBAs are going to be looking for MBA grads to round out their organizations.

In addition, consider certification programs. There are many programs available. SHRM provides some excellent programs. World at Work is the recognized expert in providing certifications for compensation and benefits professionals. There are also numerous certifications for human resource generalists and organization development experts, including MBTI (Myers-Briggs Type Indicator), PDI Profiler (Personnel Decisions, Inc.), and many more (see Appendix B). In addition, many universities, through their extension programs, provide extraordinary certification programs designed for working professionals.

THE ENVIRONMENT(S) IN WHICH YOU WANT TO WORK

There are also a number of environmental factors that impact your pursuit of your calling in HR: geography, industry, company size, company quality (A Player companies versus B or C Player companies), working inside a company, or working as a consultant as an external practitioner. And that breaks down even more. In the consulting world, you can work in a small specialized firm, a big consulting firm, or as an independent contractor. Each of these, too, have tradeoffs. As you understand what those tradeoffs are, you'll be better prepared to build your career over time to take advantage and appreciate the benefits, knowing full well that they come with a downside—which you might want to consider ways of neutralizing in your next round of changes and choices.

Geography

Your opportunities may be limited to your ability to commute or relocate for prime opportunities. Be pragmatic about what you want and what you are willing to commit to. There may be times in your life when relocation is less possible because of aging parents or young children. If you happen to be in a small town without a large, corporate profile, your chances for the fast track to a senior vice president spot in a Fortune 500 company may be limited. *For the time being.* Remember, careers can last anywhere from twenty to forty years. If you happen to be reading this book right out of school or at another key transition time in your life when all your variables are thrown up in the air, lucky you! Do your homework. Research the geographic area you are interested in for whatever reasons: Corporate environment, size, lifestyle, industry focus, even great skiing or golf (resorts need HR professionals too). And then target your career efforts on the best industries and companies within your selected geographic range.

If you are reading this book while you're still committed to whatever geographic environment you happen to be in at the moment, remind yourself why you're there. Remember that your priorities are making this location your best option at the moment. And acknowledge the value of doing what you're doing where you're doing it. If in the meantime wanderlust is beginning to reveal itself to you, use this time to leisurely explore other geographic areas (perhaps on vacation or visiting during a conference). That way, when the time comes to make your next big geographic choice, you'll already be equipped with a new list of possibilities—and the contacts to go with them (which you will read about later in the book).

Industry

Choose an industry with a future. Being the VP of HR of the best buggy whip company in the country wouldn't have meant much after the automobile replaced horses as the primary means of transportation. Are the industries you are interested in in the early stages of development with bright futures or have they peaked and headed for decline? Likewise, resist the temptation to follow the pack to the so-called "hot" industries. Once *Business Week* or *U.S. News and World Report* identify the top ten or hundred hot fields to be in within the next several years, there's a glut on the market of fresh graduates, all of whom put aside their true passions to pursue what seemed to be a good thing. So consider the alternative question: What industries provide products and services that especially interest you or that you believe in or are passionate about? Follow your passion, but be smart about it (especially if you're passionate about buggy whips). And follow your smarts, but be sure you don't leave your passion behind when you make your industry choices.

Company Size

If possible, getting experience in a multi-billion-dollar global company early in your career is the best choice. It provides an opportunity to familiarize yourself with sophisticated programs and methodologies available in bigger companies that you can apply in a variety of environments later in your career. That kind of experience also best positions you to be attractive for the top executive positions later on in your career, even if you spend a middle portion of your career in smaller companies. But more often than not, search committees want someone who has "been there, done that." And the more recently the better.

However, throughout the world, the biggest economic engine is still the small business. If you are happiest in smaller environments that feel more friendly, more creative, more turn-on-a-dime, then by all means, build a great career in that segment. Just know that that's where you will be. Make the most of that bucket of experiences. And remember the enjoyment and sense of belonging or accomplishment you got from those positions during those brief moments of frustration or envy when you see a classmate on a *Fortune* leadership panel or weighing in on some major business news development on CNN.

Internal Position

Most HR professionals build their careers inside companies. They may begin in a specialty area, maybe later move to a different specialty area, become a generalist, and move up the career ladder—maybe even crisscrossing into lateral positions as they go. There are many choices that can be made along the way. And maybe sometime later in your career you could even decide to transition your expertise to an external consulting role. As an insider you enjoy many advantages that consultants miss out on. In addition to the collaborative companionship and camaraderie of large teams of co-workers, you also enjoy the prestige of being associated with a brand-name company—especially if it's an A Player. You don't have to repeatedly establish yourself and your position when simply mentioning PepsiCo or Southwest Airlines or Microsoft will make people return your calls.

Consulting

Often, great HR folks will come to me and say, "I really want to be a consultant. I want to work less, have more balance in my life, and make more money. Wouldn't that be wonderful?" Not likely! In the consulting world you not only have to know how to *do* the work, you have to be able to *get* the work. (This can be especially hard for many HR practitioners, who think they are extroverted, only to find out they are introverted when it comes to asking for business.) Depending on the form of consulting that you might choose, you can enhance your strengths as a content expert and mitigate some of whatever weaknesses you might have in getting out and about selling your wares by joining an established consulting practice:

SMALL SPECIALIZED CONSULTING FIRMS. You could join a small group—often locally. Sometimes these smaller firms are real companies, or sometimes they work more like consortiums—virtual networking groups helping one another out. In these firms, your ability to bring in the business will be critical to your success. But at least you will have the moral support of your colleagues who can show you how it's done while you develop your own practice.

LARGE CONSULTING FIRMS. There are a number of great human resource consulting firms with solid reputations, including, to mention just a few, Hewitt Associates, Towers Perrin, Aon, and Mercer. In these companies, the firm's reputation often sells the work. Your ability to deliver the work and build great client relationships will be essential to your success. However, you will have unparalleled support in the form of your association with a high-prestige company (complete with its own marketing and advertising professionals, tools, and world-class research departments). The downside, of course, is the tremendous amount of travel time often required. If your family would rather have you home, you may not be happy inside a larger consultancy.

These large consulting firms also expect you to add to the body of knowledge. You will be expected to produce original information, data, and case studies. And your success will depend on your track record for speaking and publishing as well. This is a high-pressure environment in which only the ultra-dedicated and ambitious do well. If you're looking at consulting as an option that will allow you more flexibility, this won't be your best option.

INDEPENDENT CONTRACTOR. For many human resource professionals, this is the most difficult to pull off. To be successful, you have to be extremely well networked, have a stellar reputation for delivery on your commitments, be able to market yourself and your services, be able to build strong relationships with clients to assure repeat business, and be able to deliver great product or service. While you are doing this, you need to continually be upgrading your skills and the products that you deliver and taking care of the business matters such as invoicing, collections, public relations, and taxes. You need to be supremely well-organized, self-motivated, disciplined, and well-read. While you won't feel the same pressure to produce ground-breaking research as you would in a larger company, you must be completely current with all the developments in your field. And you must be able to write and speak about them to promote your own business. Are you ready for this challenge?

HUMAN RESOURCE ORGANIZATIONS

It helps to understand how human resource functions organize themselves as you begin to plan your career path. Although there are numerous variations, most human resource functions are organized along two basic models—the Functional Model or the Business Partner Model.

Figure 2.1 shows the Functional Model, which is more common in smaller organizations.

Figure 2.1. The Functional Model.

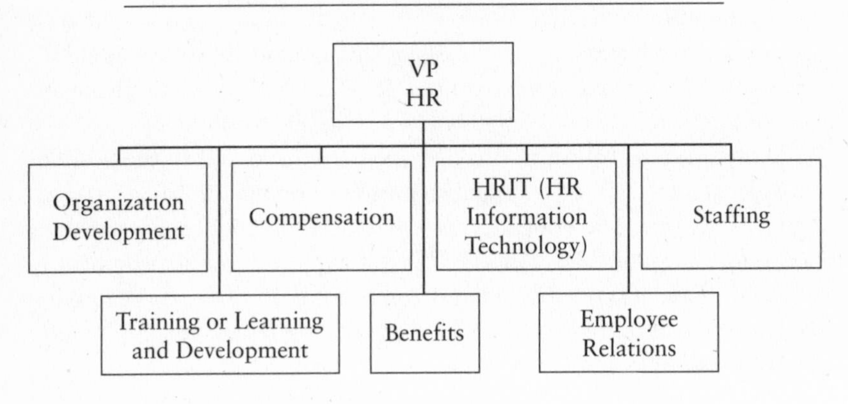

Sometimes functions will be combined. For example, Compensation, Benefits, and HRIT will often be organized under a single manager or director. A recent trend I see is to combine Staffing and Training (also called Learning and Development) into a single function called Talent Acquisition and Development. Functions also are organized or structured around specialty areas.

Larger companies may have either Functional organizations or, more common today, the Business Partner Model, which is illustrated in Figure 2.2.

In the Business Partner model, corporate specialty functions are generally responsible for development of programs. The HR generalist positions provide input on behalf of the line organization's needs to the corporate functions and roll out programs developed by the corporate functions to the line. For example, Compensation will design the salary structures and bonus programs. And although the human resource generalists are responsible for working with the corporate groups to assure that program designs incorporate the line organizations' needs, they are chartered with implementing the programs in their line organizations. HR generalists also work at a strategic level with the client group they support on matters such as workforce planning and design of organizational structures.

Figure 2.2. Business Partner Model.

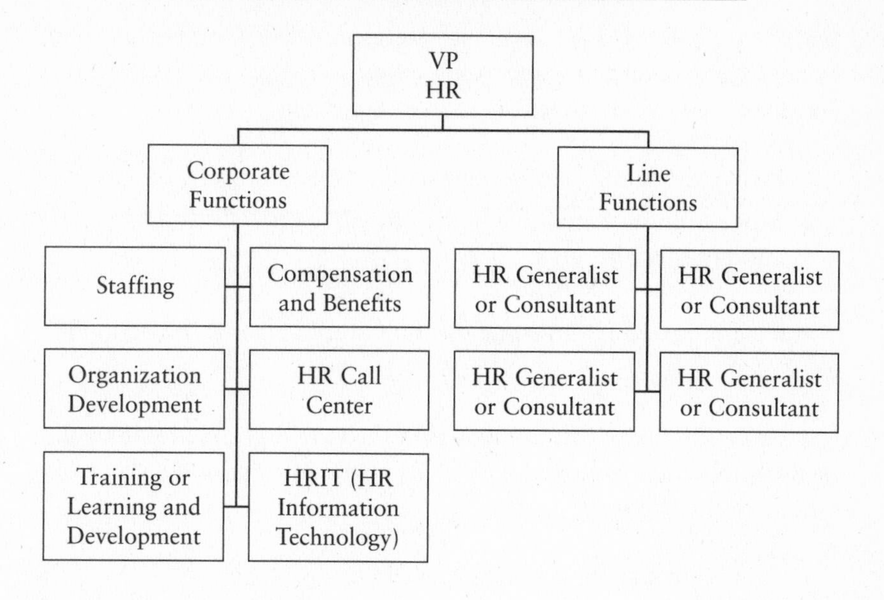

PLANNING YOUR CAREER PATH

Let's look at a couple of examples of how you might want to consider planning your career—in both the short-term and mid-term. To begin, think in terms of the career assessment model shown in Figure 2.3. Take a good look at what you have in your career kit today and what you will need to get to wherever you want to be.

Figure 2.3. Career Assessment Model.

	Today	***3 to 5 Years***	***10 Years***
Position:			
	Skills and Experiences I have in my Career Kit now	Skills and Experiences I need to add to my Career Kit beginning today	Skills and Experiences I need to add to my Career Kit long term

Example #1

Mary's long-term goal is to be a vice president of HR for a Fortune 500 company. She is currently a recruiter. From where she is right now, she may have a couple of routes to consider as options. She could

1. Prepare herself for a staffing manager or director role, or
2. Move from staffing into a human resource generalist role or another specialist area.

A filled-in career assessment indicating Mary's plans is shown in Figure 2.4.

Because she knows it's unlikely that she would be able to move directly from a staffing director role to a vice president position, she maps out her future this way:

1. Move into a staffing manager role (3 to 5 years).
2. Then move into a human resource generalist role (3 to 5 years).
3. Then *attempt* to move to a VP HR role. If the time still isn't right at this point, she may change to a larger company, which would give her a greater variety of exposures or perhaps even international experience. Or she could invest a few more years in another specialist slot, such as compensation, to get closer to the business concerns of the company and understand firsthand the financial impact of compensation programs on the business.

By her doing this, Mary's résumé would show depth of experience in at least two human resource areas, Staffing and Generalist roles. She would then look at other requirements for a VP HR slot and possibly consider doing a certification in compensation (possibly the CCP offered by World at Work). She might also consider, if she does not have an advanced degree, pursuing her master's degree, maybe in organization development or, even better, an MBA, so she can acquire a broader understanding of the nature of the business as a whole.

Ten years from now, Mary would be well-positioned with a master's, her CCP certification, and at least ten years' experience with depth in both staffing and HR generalist capacities. Isn't that better than simply meandering through your career hoping things will happen if you buckle down, work hard, and do a good job?

Figure 2.4. Mary's Career Assessment.

	Today	***3 to 5 Years***		***10 Years***
Position:	***Recruiter***	***Staffing Manager***	***HR Generalist***	***VPHR***
	Great recruiting skills and experience. Recruited all levels of employees, including manufacturing operators and administrative, engineering, and marketing professionals, up to and including senior executives.	Management experience, including hire, train, and manage performance of a recruiting team. Develop and successfully implement recruitment plans. Manage programs including college, immigration, and relocation. Budget responsibility.	Provide HR generalist support to one or more line groups. Handle significant employee relations investigations through to resolution. Obtain international experience.	Complete MBA. Complete CCP.

Example #2

Bob thinks that, long term, he may want to pursue a vice president of HR role, but he is not sure just yet. He is currently a compensation analyst, and he does love compensation work. He, too, has a number of routes to consider. He could

1. Prepare himself for a compensation manager or director role.
2. Expand his area beyond compensation into the benefits and HRIT areas, maybe eventually becoming the director of compensation, benefits, and HRIT.
3. Move from compensation into an HR generalist role.

Let's say Bob has decided that he really loves compensation and wants to expand his knowledge into the benefits and HRIT areas. Long term, he may still want to be a vice president. So he doesn't want to close any doors. But for the time being, he really prefers to stay in compensation and qualify for higher positions in the compensation specialty.

Bob's research indicates that a compensation director role would require

1. A bachelor's degree in business or related area; a master's or an MBA is almost always preferred, especially by the larger companies.
2. Experience having designed, installed, and administered a variety of compensation plans, including salary ranges, broadband pay systems, performance management and merit pay programs, incentive/bonus programs, sales commission plans, executive pay plans, and stock programs.

Thus Bob's career assessment would look like Figure 2.5.

Bob has designed, installed, and administered salary ranges, performance management/merit pay programs, and incentive/bonus plans. In addition, although he has not actually designed and installed executive pay plans and stock programs himself, he has administered them. So he does have some experience with them, and he knows people who would be happy to mentor him through the design process.

Now Bob can begin addressing the gaps:

BROADBAND PAY SYSTEMS. Bob has no experience in this area. He could begin by researching broadband systems. He could meet and dis-

Figure 2.5. Bob's Career Assessment.

	Today	*3 to 5 Years*	*10 Years*
Position:	***Compensation Analyst***	***Compensation Director***	***Compensation, Benefits and HRIT Director***
	Salary ranges Performance management/Merit pay programs Incentive/bonus plan design and implementation	Sales compensation design and implementation Executive compensation design Stock plan design Broadband systems	Complete CCB (benefits certification) HRIT experience Complete MBA

cuss the benefits of the systems with compensation professionals in other companies that have broadband systems in place. He could then, if appropriate, introduce the concept to his company. If not appropriate, he could possibly take a course in designing broadband systems or read books and technical journals on the topic to increase his knowledge in this area.

SALES COMMISSION PLANS. Bob has no experience in this area either. His company does have a sales organization. He could talk with his manager about the possibility of getting involved with developing and improving the sales commission program. He could begin to build relationships with the sales executives and reach out to help them with their plans. He could also take a course on designing sales compensation plans.

EXECUTIVE COMPENSATION AND STOCK PROGRAMS. Bob has minimal exposure to executive pay and stock plans. He has administered the existing plans but has not been involved in the design and installation phases. He could talk with his boss about expanding his role in these areas. He could take classes on the subject. He could also begin reading the annual reports and shareholder meeting notices of his company and its competitors. He could, using existing survey data and the information he collects from the competitive information, prepare a competitive analysis to begin his conversation with his boss about expanding his role in these areas.

BENEFITS AND HRIT. In the benefits area, Bob could begin taking classes to increase his knowledge of the regulatory and legal issues. He could look for opportunities to help out the benefits group or possibly be assigned to one of the benefits task teams. He could express his interest in and spend more time with the HRIT folks as well. Again, he could talk with his boss about how he might be able to contribute in these areas. He might also consider obtaining a benefits certification, like the CBP (Certified Benefits Professional, offered by World at Work), or the CEBS (Certified Employee Benefits Specialist, offered by the International Society of Certified Employee Benefits Specialists).

DON'T LET YOUR PAST GET AWAY FROM YOU

Do you remember what you had for dinner last Wednesday? What was the price of a pound of butter compared with last year? Off the top of your head, what was your heating bill last November and how much did it go up over the two Novembers before? It's hard to call up numbers at the drop of the proverbial hat. And it's even harder to put them in any kind of useful context while you're under pressure to perform.

You're going to be asked to make some sense of your career and the decisions you've made along the way while you're on the high-pressure hot seat of a job interview. And it's a lot to ask your poor brain to serve up meaningful examples and reports from the dry, dusty archives of your memory under those conditions. That's why I urge HR professionals to keep a *career journal* in which they record all their professional accomplishments and examples of how they applied both their knowledge and their strategic savvy to benefit the company—accompanied, of course, by numerical data whenever possible, to quantify the real value to the company's bottom line.

There are a couple of reasons for keeping a career journal. First, it will be an excellent record of accomplishments when you do write or update your résumé. Second, it helps you understand from a broader perspective what you have been doing and why—better preparing you to tell the story in an organized fashion when you need to.

Your career journal is a living document that you should begin as soon as possible (even while you're in school, if you're reading this book early in your career). Each time you experience a significant event (a special company recognition award, for example), complete a challenging project, or solve a difficult problem, simply record it in your career journal, being as detailed as you possibly can. A sample career journal might be as simple as the basic grid shown in Figure 2.6.

Figure 2.6. Career Journal Format.

Company ***Date*** ***Role/Title***	***Work Completed***
	Business Reason: Project Description: Result/Outcome:

Some sample entries are shown in Figure 2.7.

Note the lessons you learned with each experience, and try to put the whole experience in a context that reflects growth in both your HR career overall and your value as a business partner. And then, unlike Anita, the candidate who couldn't put her career story into any cogent package, you'll be able to organize your thoughts, your experiences, and your value in a package that you can talk about that will be irresistible to recruiters and hiring committees.

Figure 2.7. Sample Career Journal Entries.

Company ***Date*** ***Role/Title***	***Work Completed***
ABC Inc. 5/01 Compensation Director	*Business Reason:* Revenues through distribution sales had begun to level out and minimal sales growth could be achieved through this channel. To continue to grow revenues, it was necessary for the company to add a direct sales force to the company's current distribution network. The objective was to grow the direct sales from $0 to $10M in 2002, $30M in 2003, and $50M in 2004. *Project Description:* Working directly with the EVP of sales, researched and designed a competitive compensation system for a direct sales organization, allowing the company to attract and retain the talent needed to expand revenues. *Result/Outcome:* The company was able to achieve $10M revenue from direct sales in 2002 and is on track to achieve the 2003 objective.

Figure 2.7. Sample Career Journal Entries, Cont'd.

Company ***Date*** ***Role/Title***	***Work Completed***
DEF Inc. 6/02 Organization Development Consultant	*Business Reason:* Organizational transformation led by new CEO and new group VP to align organization to new business model critical to the corporate strategy. *Project Description:* Guided VPs in organization structure redesign process, designed role clarification process for VP off-site on implementation of business unit structure; created leadership transition plan for group VP; successfully facilitated business-challenge team focusing on emerging technology and new markets; designed working sessions for key project teams to streamline processes; built coaching relationships with leadership newly oriented to value of organization development. *Result/Outcome:* Designed and facilitated global leadership conferences focused on strategic planning that contributed to achievement of key business objectives; implemented change frameworks that effectively managed multiple levels of change; coached leaders and managers.

Company ***Date*** ***Role/Title***	***Work Completed***
GHI Inc. 1/00 Human Resource Director	*Business Reason:* Employee turnover in critical areas had reached significant levels (>25 percent), costing the company an estimated $2.5M in recruitment and training costs in addition to morale issues. *Project Description:* Created and implemented company-wide retention toolkit for managers, addressing communication, compensation, goal alignment, and development aspects of managing retention issues. *Result/Outcome:* Employee turnover was reduced to <20 percent in 2000, saving the company an estimated $500,000; <15 percent in 2001 with a cost savings of an additional $620,000.

Figure 2.7. Sample Career Journal Entries, Cont'd.

Company ***Date*** ***Role/Title***	***Work Completed***
JKL, Inc. 2/03 Employee Relations Manager	*Business Reason:* Potential legal costs and damages estimated to be $1M to $10M for an existing employee relations problems needed to be minimized. *Project Description:* Investigated employee complaints with regard to harassment and discrimination in the workplace, resolving 90 percent internally with no legal or damages costs incurred. Resolved remaining outstanding complaints through negotiation, limiting cost to $400,000, including legal fees. Introduced a series of two-hour training sessions for managers on topics including harassment, discrimination, wrongful termination, and related topics. *Result/Outcome:* Successfully minimized cost of existing legal actions as a result of employee complaints. Minimized future potential legal costs by training managers to better manage employee relations problems in the workplace to avoid litigious situations.

WHAT INTERVIEWERS WILL BE LISTENING FOR

By now you should have a good idea of the entire landscape of the HR career possibilities and the many turns and choices you can make. And overall, your choices have made sense to you so far. Now your challenge is to present the story of your career to date in such a way that it makes sense to a recruiter or hiring committee. This takes an added level of insight. It's not enough to just tell your story as a series of events. You must put it in a context that is *meaningful,* not just to you, but to the person you're telling your career story to.

In any interview for a position—even in an interview with a recruiter to determine whether you're a viable candidate to consider for a position—you're in a selling role. And with any selling role, your chances of success increase immensely when you're able to see the need through the eyes of your customer—in this hypothetical case, me.

If you look at the interview encounter through my eyes, you'll see that it's not so important to me that you're a wonderful, passionate HR professional with twenty-five years' experience in a Fortune 50 company, even with that coveted track record of growth and stability. *What's important to me is the question of whether or not what you've done and who you are is what my client company is looking for.*

As we progress in our interview, there will be a subtext of questions I'll be asking *myself* while I'm asking you for information. Bear these in mind as you answer them. Then you won't be tempted to stray away from the question with some kind of wandering answer, a la poor Anita. And you'll be able to give me precisely the answer I'm looking for. This doesn't guarantee that you'll get the chance to progress to the hiring committee. But it does come awfully close to guaranteeing that, if you *are* an ideal candidate for the position, I won't inadvertently write you off the list because of confusion or lack of focus.

This is what I'll be thinking as our interview moves along:

1. *Do you have a career story that makes sense?* Do you have a plan that you're executing? Or are you meandering through your career, taking new opportunities as they present themselves, regardless of what they are? As part of my routine approach to each interview, I start at the bottom of every résumé, and with every juncture where candidates have made a change, I ask them, "Exactly what prompted that change?" I want to know what motivates them to change and if there is a pattern of planfulness that I can spot. Do you go after career moves that offer more experience and knowledge, or just more money?

2. *What projects have you actually accomplished, and do you know the business necessity behind them?* Let's say, for instance, that you developed an employee referral program. What would you say when I ask, "Why?" That it was a "cool" thing to do? That the other companies in your community or industry have one and you were feeling behind the times without one? Or that you were experiencing difficulty recruiting certain kinds of employees and that you were incurring $20,000 per hire agency fees. Over the previous year you had discovered that 95 percent of the employees who were referred to the company by friends who already worked there tended to stay longer and the cost of recruiting them was only $2,000. Which answer do you think would prompt me to present you as a viable candidate to my client?

I am always listening for indications that you know enough about your business overall to understand the business need behind your activities and that you can tie your accomplishments to solving that larger business problem. And if you can say it in numbers, so much the better!

3. *Are you wise enough to admit you don't know everything?* The irony is inescapable. When you're at the beginning of your career, you will be evaluated more by what you know than what you have done. You haven't done much more than go to school at this point, so it makes sense. But as your career matures and you progress through more seasoned ranks, recruiters and hiring committees are going to want to see how gracefully you concede what you *don't* know. I've seen too many otherwise attractive candidates sink their chances by trying to bluff their way through difficult answers or by making sweeping generalizations about the industry or specialty they hope to transition into. It's perfectly acceptable and expected for you *not* to be an expert in every aspect of the new opportunity that we're discussing. What I am most interested in hearing you talk about is how you would expect to go about finding the answers and filling in your knowledge gaps.
4. *Don't forget to be able to talk about your passion!* I want to know what excites you! Don't feel that you must stifle your excitement in order to be most attractive to the particular opportunity before us. It might not be the best opportunity for you. And it's possible that I have another opening—one that has your name written all over it. But I'll only be able to put your name to that opening if I'm able to see your total picture: Your résumé, your interests, and your plans for your career future.

You are the master of your career, and you are its chief storyteller. Manage it well. Make decisions according to your master plan. Be able to tell the story of what you have accomplished, both in terms of your own career and in terms of how you have benefited the companies you have been associated with. And you'll be able to tell a story of success in your HR career throughout your entire life.

SUMMARY

- Always be able to explain in business terms how and why you made the career choices that you did.

- Plan a career path that will lead you to the future you desire.
- Careers are long, so you will have plenty of opportunities to change direction, alter your pace of progression, and vary the mix of opportunities you intentionally collect throughout the years.
- Keep a career journal to track the story of your career. Track the quantifiable advantages that companies have been able to benefit from by having you on their team.

INTERVIEW

Mary Jean Connors

Senior Vice President, Knight Ridder

HR was the furthest career choice from Mary Jean Connors's mind when she began her working life as a newspaper journalist. However, as she progressed through the normal channels of journalism success, her management skills and talents caught the attention of the business executives of the papers she worked for. And after a lot of serious thought and many conversations with trusted advisors, she made the jump to the corporate side of the "fourth estate."

As senior vice president, she runs the people side of Knight Ridder, the second-largest newspaper company in the United States, with 18,000 employees, thirty-one dailies, twenty-six non-daily papers, and eighty-three regional websites. In this interview she discusses how human resources has changed over the breadth of her career so far, just as journalism has.

What is the best piece of advice you have ever received?

I had a boss, Janet Chusmir, who was the editor of the *Miami Herald* back in the days when there were very few women editors. I think she was one of the first female editors of a large urban newspaper. It was very liberating to work for her, and she made me feel that I did belong after all. And even though I ended up at corporate and she continued on as editor, we remained friends.

She died suddenly at 61, right after she had decided to retire. When I was at her home after the funeral, I said to her husband, "I just don't know what I'm going to do. My role model has died." And then he said, "Maybe it's time for *you* to be the role model."

Others had prepared me. Janet had prepared me. And now I realized, "Hey! It's time! You're a grown-up. It's time for you to own your career, to *realize* that you own your career and realize that others are looking at you as the role model." It was a rite of passage—a sad way to go through it, but it was a rite of passage all the same.

At some point in your life, you have to realize that you have to start owning [your journey] yourself and not look for anyone else to show you the path. Now *you* have to be the pathfinder and create the path for others. People are starting to watch you. You can either be a force for good or not. What model are you going to leave for others?

I suppose we all wake up one day and start thinking about "What legacy will I leave? What will people learn from watching my career and how I behave?" You have the sense of responsibility to a broader world than just your own career.

What was the moment your career changed forever?

I was humming along in a journalism career and very happy as the assistant managing editor at the *Miami Herald.* Then the senior vice president for the new corporate Knight Ridder asked me to come up and be his executive assistant. Those roles were designed to help people advance their careers and expose them to the whole corporation. The invitation was sold to me as "maybe one day running my own newsroom." I was very honored, and I thought the world of him. And Janet very much encouraged me to do it.

In this new role, I got involved in other things that were broader than the newsroom, and I began to think of a broader career beyond the newsroom. They were looking for a vice president for human resources for the *Philadelphia Inquirer and Daily News,* which was by far the biggest newspaper Knight Ridder has. Tony Ridder and others suggested that maybe I should go do that because it would give me exposure to the business side in an operating environment.

Janet advised me not to do it, and so I said to them, "No, I'm a journalist." To which they said, "Why don't you just go look?" I went to look, and I was very intrigued. It was either that or go back to a newsroom. And even though I hadn't been the editor, I had been assistant managing editor of a major newspaper. I had done all the different departments. And I found myself to be much more intrigued than I wanted to be with this new opportunity. My husband was back home saying, "Don't do this." Janet was so against it she even got *her* husband on the phone to tell me it was a bad idea. But I just couldn't let go of it. It just intrigued me so much.

So I went to Philadelphia as the vice president of human resources. I really loved it. There are crises every day. I played a role in very intimate ways in fixing problems and making a difference. My husband moved. Then I got a call less than one year later from the CEO at the time, saying, "Tony and I are looking for someone to run human resources for the entire corporation." And so then I came back to Miami to talk to them about it.

This was the big deciding moment. Not only was I going to leave the newsroom, I was going to leave the operating environment altogether. I was going to be in corporate. I had to think about what it is that I enjoy in work and where it is that I can really make a difference. I felt that a lot of people can be good journalists, but I had a broader curiosity. And I wasn't one of those people who felt vocationally driven to the "order." I didn't feel it was a calling the way some people did. Even though I loved what newspapers do, and I still love it, I didn't feel that I was born with *journalist* written on my forehead.

I knew that where I made the most value-added contribution was helping people solve management problems and identify talent. I enjoyed and was good at helping and counseling people. That's where I really got my thrill. Because I knew journalism and had been a successful journalist, I was able to do that in the newspaper environment. It was that differentiating piece of me. And so I took the job. And that was thirteen years ago, and here I am.

Did you find your journalism background gave you a kind of credibility that you wouldn't have had otherwise?

Absolutely. Because I had been a successful journalist in one of the bigger papers, and because I had been well received in my year at the *Philadelphia Inquirer and Daily News,* I had all these contacts, all these relationships and credibility going in. It would be easier for me than for someone who was perceived as a career HR executive. God only knows I have since learned that those people often know a lot more than I do about things and can be very helpful. There was no going back though, and that was both scary and great. Once I did it, it really felt right.

Do you miss the writing life?

No. My husband continued to be a journalist. I'm surrounded by journalists, and I write a lot. Can you do a job today without writing all the time? Communication skills are one of the most important skills any person can have in a profession. I feel very lucky that I had training in it.

What is the one thing you wish you had done differently?

I really don't believe in "would have" or "should have." I think it's a waste of time. I think you should learn from the decisions you make.

Sometimes I make decisions very, very quickly. And I'm not a person to dig deeply into the details if I don't have to. Most of the time that's a plus. But every now and then it's not. Sometimes you make decisions, and there is only so much you can know and you can't look back. Sometimes when you make decisions, maybe there's something more that you could have looked at. It might have resulted in a different decision. I have made decisions like that about people and situations, when what would have made a better decision was knowable if I had just taken a little more time to talk to people or read the fine print, or just taken time to research it more.

Intuition is largely the ability to very quickly synthesize a lot of the data that you do have. But sometimes, many times, you should question and test your intuition against the facts.

What is the best piece of advice to offer those on the way up?

If it isn't something you think you would enjoy, don't do it. You have to work with people you like, trust, and respect. So any job or opportunity that would not afford you that would be a bad choice. Do things in your career and life that will open more doors, not close them. Do something that will *expand* the future. If you do those things, no matter what choices you make, you will be fine.

What do up-and-comers need now that you didn't need when starting out?

It helps nowadays to have a deeper knowledge of the law than I had coming in. I've acquired it over the years because I've had to.

A law degree is probably a great asset. But if you have the law degree—but you don't have the ability to think through issues fully and understand the business and help people see the variety of solutions they might use and how they might work—then the law degree alone is not going to make you a good HR executive. In addition, if HR executives have the opportunity to be in an operating role, they will always be richer in their ability to help people and bring more credibility to the role.

The other thing HR professionals need now more than before is judgment about people, and you get that a million ways. In a world where things are moving fast and the business changes, you have to be willing to size up the integrity, smarts, and competence of the people that your company is going to be engaging with. There is so much more riding on it today than there used to be. That ability to judge smartly about people is absolutely essential to being an HR executive today.

All these things have always been useful. I just think that the way the world has evolved, they are so much more important today than they used to be. Because the old administrative kind of work is being handled through technology and outsourcing, you can't really get by on those skills inside the company anymore. It's the more qualitative abilities that I think differentiate the HR executive today.

What is the best thing new entrants can do when they go into the profession?

Become very savvy businesspeople.

What's the worst?

Don't learn the business. Be a poor communicator. I don't think you can survive as a poor communicator today.

What characteristics and qualities do you look for when hiring an HR professional?

In addition to everything we've already talked about, I'd like to include empathy. If you're going to engage with people, you can't be a cold fish. And people can tell if you're phony. I'm looking for people who really care. Humility is a very good thing for anyone who is going to have responsibility that affects people's lives.

Humility actually comes from confidence. The really successful executives make decisions based on their own values, experience, and judgment. And they decide where they stand. The people I find who are not successful are the people who look for where to land. They wait to see where the boss is going. Or they wait to see what the prevailing opinion is. Or they defend their position even when they've made a mistake. The confident people have the humility to know when they are to say their piece no matter where the boss is going. And if it turns out that they're wrong, they also have no problem saying, "Gosh, it turns out I have something to learn here."

It's not about being right or wrong. It's about being true to what you know and the value that you can add. Sometimes you are going to be right. And sometimes wrong. The only value that you can bring is what *you* bring. And to try to pick up the signals from someone else or try to browbeat everyone through the imposition of your opinion to me is the sign of a person who is not a full leader. A full leader has to have humility and courage—both in the same package.

What was the risk that you took in your career that paid off?

I was a city editor in Cincinnati between 1979 and 1980, and I got a call from the *Miami Herald* asking me to come down to look at the newsroom. They were looking for an urban affairs editor. I had never been to Florida. I didn't know anyone in the whole city except the photo editor there. But I went down anyway. I liked the paper, and I thought I would learn a lot from the people there. I knew I would grow more than if I stayed where I was. And they offered me the job before I left. So I went home and asked myself, "Can I make it if I go do that? Or is it too big a stretch for me?" I decided I had to try. So I just showed up and started to work. I grew so much more than if I had stayed in Cincinnati. It turned out to be an extraordinary time to be in Miami and to be a journalist.

Can you ever imagine yourself doing this in another place?

I do love the newspaper business. I believe people don't leave unless they're unhappy. I've always been happy. I've been happy in the company, and I've been happy in my career. So I don't have any reason to go anywhere else.

I love the company. There are great people in the company who have done a lot for me and for the company, and I feel like I owe something. I think more about how I can give back to all of them—even to those who are gone, like Janet. How can I leave a legacy? How can I give back? I've worked for wonderful people who have really cared deeply. And who really did take the leadership of the company and the preservation of quality journalism as a mission—even in tough times. It's an honor to be part of that.

3

THE POWER OF THE PLANNED TRANSITION

This chapter helps you make the most of the transition process itself, as you prepare to leave one company or position and seek out new, career-building opportunities.

SINCE YOU ARE HOLDING this book, chances are excellent that you're anticipating a change in your career coming up soon. It may be imminent (maybe you actually resigned yesterday, or maybe you hope to soon). Or maybe you're just about to enter the HR profession and you want to get some sense of the career landscape before making your first choice. No matter what your circumstances, if you're motivated to take your next step according to some long-term vision of how all your decisions will compile over time, you're already well ahead of your colleagues.

It's no wonder that the essential ingredients to a successful long-term HR career have been a mystery until recently. Historically, HR has been a profession that people wander into and meander through, driven by happenstance—changes in industrial currents or shifts in the economic winds. Until recent years, very few people actually planned to create an HR *career.* We've been so focused on acquiring the skills and knowledge required to be truly successful at our profession that no one has really stopped to codify the steps necessary to build a leadership-bound career in HR over the course of an HR professional's entire working life. As with almost every other career path, the overall mystique of "just lucky, I guess," or "right time, right place" is all too often the stock answer when people are asked how they have achieved their success.

As a recruiter I can tell you right now that, when I get an assignment to help fill an opening in HR, not one search requisition has specified, "Bring us someone who was at the right place at the right time." And no successful candidate landed the offer because he or she said, "Just lucky, I guess." Search committees ask for very specific accomplishments in very specific corporate environments. And they want candidates who know not only what they're doing but also where they're going.

What kinds of positions you want to be eligible for is entirely up to you. In Chapter 2, I provided specifics about how you plot your steps and choices to achieve the results you desire. In addition, you will find some very useful forms to help you think about your career options in Appendix A, Career Preparation Self-Assessment. You must be grounded in the conviction that, no matter where you are in your career, you are absolutely in control over the choices you make, how you make them, and when you make them. So here I hope to implant that sense of power and help you understand how to make the most of every choice and change you make.

Your career can be planned and managed to produce extraordinary results for both you and the companies you associate with over time. Even if circumstances produce bumps along the way (and they will), you can control your destiny. No matter where you go—up, sideways, down, even out for a little while—you have the power to make planned transitions that will lead you to the next step. And by the time you reach the end of your working life, you can look back and say to yourself, "Yes, that's pretty much the way I planned it."

REASONS FOR YOUR NEXT CHANGE

Search committees almost universally ask me to bring them only candidates whose track records reflect stability and progressive growth in their careers and skill sets. Growth is change, and if there ever were a time in this history of *homo sapiens,* now is the time to make friends with the prospect of change for the rest of your working life. If you're old enough to be reading this book, you're old enough to remember a time when things were completely different. Even if you're a Generation Next'er, you remember a time when your older brother, sister, or neighbor entered a job market in which money and opportunities were being thrown at them. Things are a little different now, aren't they?

Like it or not, know it or not, there's a change on your horizon. And it could be a marvelously positive one that's going to propel you to a new lifestyle of satisfaction, fun, and fascinating work. Some of the positive reasons for a change ahead of you are now discussed.

Personal desires and circumstances have changed. Maybe you just graduated from college and are ready to take your first job. Now, there's a change. Or family circumstances—a new marriage, a new baby, you're a trailing spouse—are telling you that yesterday's job isn't going to cut it in your own personal Tomorrowland. Or maybe you are still happy with your current company, but you know you're ready for additional scope and responsibility. Or you want a sprucier title. Or you simply want more money.

A desire for a geographic relocation. The city where you are is okay, but you're tired of shoveling snow. Or palm trees are just too weird to behold in December. Or you want to move closer to your parents so they can pitch in and help with your new babies. Or you know that, in this era of globalism, long-term HR careers are nowhere if they don't include international experience, and your current company is strictly domestically focused.

A desire for a more exciting company or industry sector. Maybe you want to repackage your career kit and offer it to a company whose products and mission are something that you're really passionate about. Or you want an employer that can expose you to more current technology or more *now* methodologies. Or you know that you're now ready for the so-called A Player company. You've built up both your confidence and your skill set and you're ready to take it to the "Big Time."

Sometimes you're just plain ready to move on. You don't need a better reason than that. Just make sure that your transition plan is already in place before that lovely little itch of "needing to move on" has inflamed into "*get me outta here!*" Desperation is not a good position to be negotiating from. So pay attention to the little itches that seem almost too inconsequential to notice—they may be just the advance warning that it's time to put your next plan into action.

And now for the negative reasons. *These are signs that your career is about to derail.* If you notice them early enough, you will still have the luxury of taking your next steps according to plan. Eventually, you will feel that sense of urgency (unless you've already been snapped up by your next great employer). If urgency arises, it will be less agonizing if you can console yourself with the knowledge that your career search is already well underway.

However you experience this evidence that it's time to push on, whatever you do, don't despair! It happens to more people than you know. Some of the warning signs are discussed below:

You're out of the loop. Suddenly you're no longer being invited to meetings that once included you and your insights. You're hearing about decisions after they have already been made instead of being consulted beforehand.

Business is bad. Suddenly your boss is avoiding contact with you. You're being asked to assemble lay-off packages, and you're seeing your immediate colleagues on the list. Business is shaky; market conditions have outpaced your company's ability to deliver.

Prime projects are being given to others. You're no longer getting the plum assignments you used to get regularly. You don't know why, and no one is interested in giving you a credible answer or advice on how to get back on that track.

You have a new boss and he or she likes to hire his or her own people, or your peers are being promoted around you. These speak volumes.

When these signs of derailment rear their ugly head, it's more than time to evaluate your situation honestly. (Remember, you're always in the best negotiating position when you're still employed.) Ask yourself: "Do I want to stay here? Do I want to do what it takes to stay here? Can I turn this situation around in a reasonable amount of time? Is this negative situation a matter of circumstances? Or is it me? If it's me, can I fix it?"

Whatever you do, don't take it personally. It's not about your worthiness as a human being or whether you deserve to be gainfully employed or lucky in some overall cosmic sense. Bad news happens, and the longer you stay in your career, the longer you will be exposed to the possibility that some unpleasant turn of events will cause you to look around for something new. It's not about you. Or it might be about you. Only you can really know the difference.

TAKE CARE OF THE PATH YOU'RE ON

Once you've finally made your decision, the process of making the decision itself has moved you along to a new point on your career journey. If your decision is to stay, some transition has occurred, even if it's a resolution to "stick it out." Whether you stay or go, there is some new housekeeping that needs to be done. All your relationships have been transformed, however slightly. And your sense of self-awareness has shifted as well. New terms must be established.

Just because those relationships and responsibilities are now relegated to yesterday, that doesn't mean that they should go ignored. If you decide to leave your job, you want to leave matters well-tended. Whether it is a desk full of projects or contacts, you want to leave everything in such a way that you can continue positive relationships with all the people you have been working with, especially your boss.

There are many ways to tell your boss that you're ready to move on so that the news can actually enhance your relationship, not threaten it.

If you have a good, trusting, mutually supportive relationship with your boss, you can even tell him or her well in advance that you have decided to be receptive to opportunities, should they come along.

"I have really enjoyed this position I'm in right now and am learning so much," you might say, "but I'd like my next position to be one where I can actually run a department. What do you think I can do to position myself to be the most qualified if such an opportunity were to come along? And could you keep your eyes open for opportunities that might help groom me for that next career move?"

If you have an open relationship where there's trust and respect, this kind of news tells your boss where you'd like to be heading in the near future. It doesn't mean you're quitting now, next week, or even next month. It just has a "whenever" timeframe attached to it. And you're inviting your boss to be your most important mentor, biggest advocate, and most valuable partner in helping you achieve your goals.

That might not mean that your boss will help you directly or even immediately. If you're a wonderful employee, he or she might not want to lose you. But this kind of conversation establishes a tone for a long-term relationship that will last long after this particular era of employment is behind you both.

(Don't expect your boss, for instance, to offer your name to recruiters when they call. It's rare for bosses to give recruiters their own people. And from a recruiter's point of view, if I didn't know the boss, that kind of recommendation might make me suspicious. But at a later time—remember that careers are long—if they hear of opportunities that are right for you, they'll send them your way. Or they'll recommend you to inquiring recruiters.)

There's no shame or disloyalty implied in wanting to push on, either ASAP or eventually. Human resources is a profession, and professionals know other professionals want and need to grow their careers. Not only is that all right, it should be expected. A boss who thinks his or her employee has no ambition to develop is the one who should be concerned.

Don't throw your newly designed future in the faces of your co-workers. No one likes to be left behind, and it's understandable that your current co-workers may be envisioning your new position as the cushy new spot in the Emerald City while they're stuck in Mudville. On the other hand, false modesty, of course, will make you look smug and insincere. Even if you've decided to leave but haven't announced your decision yet, be mindful of the attitude you project. There are few characters more unattractive than the co-worker who has already departed in his or her heart.

In your own mind, these co-workers may already begin to feel like shades of an increasingly distant or irrelevant past. But in fact, they are the foundation of a network that you will be drawing from—and contributing to—for the rest of your working life. Treat them like gold. You'll be seeing them again one day, perhaps as members of a future search committee that will be considering you for the job of your dreams.

TAKE CARE OF THE PATH GOING FORWARD

You've given it some serious thought and now you know for sure that you will be wanting to push on some time soon. You haven't run screaming out the door, yelling, "Take this job and shove it!" Nor have you been fired (emergency job searching is an entirely different book). You have made this decision at leisure, and you know you have some time to take your next step planfully and mindfully. Or maybe you're a college senior and it's February. You know you have three to six months to find your first job before the new guest-room furniture your parents ordered will arrive. A rule of thumb for job seekers is that it will take around a month of searching for every $10,000 that you expect to earn. Obviously, that rule of thumb is subject to a variety of variables such as the economy and your expectations (if you're a new college grad, for instance, and expect to be making $100,000 with your first job, you can expect to be looking a very long time).

Even if you have to endure the intolerable job you already have for a short period of time, consider that endurance trial an investment in your future. You never want to be in a position where you have to take a bad job knowingly just because you need that paycheck. If you're feeling the urgency to seek a new situation for whatever reason, try to accept the idea that you should budget at least three months to find your next fantastic opportunity. And don't be discouraged if it takes longer.

Regardless of your hurry for finding your next new career move, having a timeline will help you design your immediate future so that you will take intentional action that will lead you to your next best position.

If You Have Three Months

Review your career journal, noting and making a list of your most important accomplishments in your recent jobs. The more senior you are in the organization, the more prepared you must be to talk about your achievements in terms of how they benefited the organization overall. The more you can speak in quantifiable terms the better. If you are just entering the HR field or have only been in it for a couple of years, be prepared to speak in terms of projects you were an important team member for and what individual assignments you took from start to finish. Also list the ideas you had that would have benefited the company—even if the ideas weren't actually actionable or adopted, your ability to generate innovative approaches to organizational challenges will be a big plus to hiring authorities.

Make the most of the time that's left where you are. If you're still in school, participate in every networking event that is available to you. Go to your local SHRM chapter meetings. Try to design some kind of survey or research project that will put you in front of your area's leading employers. Even if you don't intend to stay in that town after graduation, it's valuable to start networking where you are and practice having business meetings and interviews in a low-stakes situation.

If you're further along in your career, you should also go to SHRM (or other local professional group) meetings and volunteer as much as you can on committees and special projects. Look for opportunities to have face-to-face meetings with your targeted employers and say yes to every chance to meet someone new.

Of course, make sure your résumé is completely updated and ready to distribute to those who ask. Be judicious about who actually receives your résumé. This is not a numbers game; it's a process in which you will benefit by being as discerning as your prospective employers are. Be careful not to float your résumé around too much. If your résumé starts showing up in all the likely spots (the on-line job boards, stacks of résumés applying for a wide variety of jobs, job fairs, for instance), you may look too available. And you will run the risk of your boss—or one of his friends—seeing your résumé in circulation. If you happen to see a job opening that appeals to you at a desirable company, don't just send your résumé to the same post office box or email address that everyone else will be sending theirs to. Find someone who already works in that company and ask for an introduction. If you don't know someone already, you probably know someone who knows someone. If you don't, take a good look at your networking skills and habits.

Identify companies that you especially want to work with. See if you can find someone there who is willing to do an informational interview. If you're a SHRM member, for instance, look at the SHRM directory and see if there are members who work at your target companies. Contact them and introduce yourself as a fellow SHRM member. That's an important commonality that should net you at least a few minutes of phone time, if not an informational interview, which is your main objective. Try to get as many target companies as you can so you don't inadvertently send out a feeling of ultra-high pressure to your new contacts as you meet them.

Don't let your perceived lack of experience hold you back. Sometimes your passion will give you the edge you need to land a job that others think is out of their reach. When I was teaching a class on recruiting at the University of Santa Cruz one year, there were two students sitting in the front row. One had great experience already—a couple or three years. The other one had remotely related experience. She had worked in a college placement office that basically just told students where to go to look for jobs. One evening I brought in a staffing manager from Cisco Systems as a guest speaker for my class. The student who had the lesser experience, but far more confidence, approached him.

"You know, Cisco is a wonderful place," she said. "I'd love to talk to you about my background and see if you have some career advice for me."

She met with him, he gave her some career advice, and he ended up hiring her at Cisco for a recruiter job that the other student was probably far more qualified to do.

If you have a good background, a good résumé, and a solid skill set and you're honest about your intentions, knowledgeable people will at least give you a few moments of their time. If you're not used to talking to total strangers and are worried about getting tongue-tied, simply say something like: "I'm currently in XXX position at my company and I'm exploring what my logical next best steps might be. I realize you don't have any new jobs posted and, as a matter of fact, I'm perfectly comfortable where I am. One of my career goals is to become an HR manager, and I was wondering if I could invite you for a cup of coffee and we could talk. I'd especially like to know what I can be doing in my career so that I would eventually become a more attractive candidate down the road."

Remember to return the favor. If you are looking at only a short three-month horizon, you might be feeling too edgy to give someone else professional advice at the moment. But remember that every opportunity to meet someone new is also an opportunity to meet someone who is connected by association to thousands of other people. Likewise, if you get a phone call from a recruiter looking to fill a position that is unrelated to your ambitions, give that person some of your time anyway. Many HR professionals keep a file of résumés or a list of others they know are looking in a desk drawer. Whenever I call, they're ready to share names.

When they call me, you can bet I'll find time to talk with them. Even though recruiters aren't in the business of helping people find jobs (they're in the business of helping their client companies find and select from a small group of elite candidates for specific openings), the better recruiters may be willing to take some time for you. But recruiters will take and return the phone calls of people they know already much more quickly than calls from strangers. If they don't already have a relationship with you, they'll likely only want to know if your credentials match the criteria for a position that's currently on their desk. If not, they may wait until they do before getting back to you. Lesson: Build your relationships before you need them!

Consultants and other vendors are master networkers. They have to be. They have to grow their own businesses and they're out in the field more than you are. If you're on good, personal terms with any of these external service providers, let them know that you would be open to hearing about any positions they might know of. In the meantime, if there are openings in your current company, let them know of the opportunities so they can pass on the good news to their other contacts. It helps them, it helps total strangers who may become your grateful evangelists, and it helps you. It's all about connecting.

Consider teaching. Local universities, their extension programs, and seminar providers are always looking for guest lecturers and regular faculty members who have real-life business experience they can draw from. Don't think you might be too young or new in the profession to be able to offer anything relevant. It's common for schools to invite their recent alumni to return to the classroom to give current students a firsthand peek at the experiences that wait for them their first year out in the job market. Teaching and speaking publicly adds credibility to your background and boosts your visibility tremendously. You never know who is in your classroom and who knows whom.

Renegotiate your relationship with your current boss. Volunteer for more projects internally. This will make your remaining time more valuable for everyone, those three months will go by faster, and your boss may see in you a more empowered, capable employee than he or she thought you were. You may get more significant projects as an incentive to stay. On the other hand, if you don't, maybe there is a message there too.

Volunteer for more community initiatives and nonprofit projects in a field that is related to your new career destination. If you have a particular company or new field picked out, try to find out in what volunteer environments its employees are most likely to be found, and show up. Not just once, but invest yourself in seeing volunteer projects all the way through. This is not about social climbing and taking advantage of real community need, but you can leverage these opportunities as great ways of joining social circles you want to be a part of. Just make sure your interest is sincere and genuine.

Assess your image. How well do you show? How well do you dress? Have you become a little sloppy as you have grown comfortable in your current position? Do you reflect today's or yesterday's news? Now is the time to inventory your appearance and other image issues from head to toe. Haircut? Check. Appropriate jewelry? Check. Grooming? Check. No gum? Check. Clothes clean, current? Check. Shoes polished and repaired? Check. Everything fits? No gaps or stretches? Check. When you look your best, you'll feel, reflect, and inspire confidence.

If You Have Six Months

In addition to everything in your three-month window, these steps will accelerate your job-search process so you build out a lengthier game plan:

Join a networking group or, if a networking group doesn't already exist in your area, start one. It doesn't have to be formal; you don't even have to have a specific reason. Just bring a number of your peers together. In *HR from the Heart,* Yahoo's Chief People Officer, Libby Sartain, talks about her Hole-in-the-Wall gang, which was made up of senior vice presidents of the major companies in the Dallas area, including her counterpart at American Airlines (she was with Southwest at the time). Sure, they talked business, but their main purpose was to get together once a month and just have fun at some greasy spoon (the greasier the better). The members of their gang have gone on to retirement or different parts of the country, but they still find each other at major conferences and their networking continues.

Make your networking group large enough to bring in the variety of perspectives and disciplines you're looking for, but small enough so that you can really get to know the group's members.

Distinguish yourself from the pack to get the attention of recruiters. Lengthen your list of publishing and speaking credits, and volunteer to appear on community panel discussions about employment and economic development issues in your area.

Take another look at your résumé. Since you have six months to position yourself for the next opportunity, what classes, training, and/or certifications can you begin to be even more qualified for your ideal next job than you were three months ago?

With six months to work with, you can make amazing transformations in your personal attributes. If you need to make significant changes that will make you feel more confident, now is the time to do it. Six months can chisel away fifteen to twenty pounds painlessly, if you budget your time wisely. A daily exercise routine will lift your spirits and put a glow of health on your face. It will also make you sleep better, which will boost the overall impression of your being relaxed and in charge of your world. If your prospects are being held back because of bad grammar, pronunciation problems, or an accent that sends the wrong signal, this is a good time to hire a vocal coach or tutor. If you smoke, give yourself these months to quit.

If You Have a Year

Do all of the above, and help yourself by being part of the solution for industry-wide problems. Put together a community or industry-wide consortium to work on a particular problem facing the industry. For example, the most recent Federal Accounting Standards Board (FASB) pending rules forcing the expensing of stock options is a hot issue at this writing. Your consortium could study the subject and make recommendations as to the industry's—or your own company's—response. As much as possible, make this a project that will appeal to a broader group of people. Your company will long be remembered as the one that took the initiative to reach out, and you could be on the radar screen of some new influential people.

Quick and Easy Steps You Can Take Today to Springboard Your HR Career

- Identify someone whose success you admire and ask that person to be your career mentor.
- Register for a major conference and your local professional group meetings. Don't let yourself back out of going.
- Update your résumé and career journal.
- Call PR and ask them how you can help promote the company as a best employer.
- Join Toastmaster's.
- Call the business department of your local college or university and volunteer to give a presentation to a class on some aspect of HR in the real world.

- Make an appointment with a career coach and/or image consultant.
- Find someone who has a job like the one you would like to have. Invite that person to lunch and ask for advice on how to achieve what he or she has accomplished.

MANAGE THE OLD RELATIONSHIPS AFTER YOU SAY GOOD-BYE

How you manage the relationships in your current company after you accept the new position could make a big difference in your future prospects many years—even decades—from now.

The first item on your agenda is to resign right. This means that you must talk to your boss in private and work together to design a way to announce your resignation. Put your old job in just as positive a light as you're putting your new opportunity.

"I've been given this great job offer that will take my career to the next level," you might say. "It was really hard to make this decision because I love this company and truly value the experience I have gained working with you here. But I'm at a point in my career where this change makes sense for me." Even if your boss knows you're lying, putting your resignation in as graceful a way as possible will create an overall feeling of "all's well that ends well" goodwill that will leave a positive impression that lasts longer than the nitty-gritty unhappy details from the past both of you would love to forget. Then decide together how you (or your boss) will make the announcement to the rest of the department and company.

Keep in mind that, when you are going in to resign, you are bringing a new set of problems along with you. How is the company going to replace you? How is it going to get your work done in the meantime? Since you've known for a long time that you were looking for a new job and have now accepted the next opportunity, you should have been giving this issue significant thought. Your last service to your old company may well be the package of solutions or at least suggested alternatives you bring with you into the meeting in which you make your announcement. Remember, be about the solution, not the problem.

A planned transition includes more than just the details of your job. It also includes the plan for how your successor can take over where you left off after you depart the company. So you should have already prepared for this, and now all you have to do is roll it out in the form of a suggested transition plan. Show your boss that you've put thought into how it might be handled; even suggest some names of a few people you think are qualified to be promoted into your place. If you are a leader, one of your lasting legacies—especially in the field of HR—is that you grow great people to take your place. Now is the time to demonstrate that. Or maybe you can recommend some great people outside your company for your job.

However your boss decides to manage the transition, cooperate with him or her to do the smoothest job possible. Document everything: your procedures, what you do, what you've left undone, where projects stand, your key contacts and their phone numbers, and so on.

PLAN TO HELP OTHERS AS YOU SETTLE IN

Powerful, planned transitions include making sure that you remember your friends. As you start getting busy with your new job, it's natural to feel that you don't have the time or mental bandwidth to think about anything other than demonstrating your true value to your new company's HR needs.

As someone who has been in the job market for three months to a year, you have heard of more opportunities than ever before and have met more people who are also searching than ever before. For every job that has passed you by—or that you have said no to—you have had the opportunity to increase your own network of warm contacts of grateful colleagues and recruiters.

Don't let the terrific fact that you're now working to settle in to your next job keep you from performing like a powerful connector to help other people who know you continue their own career climb as well. Who knows, after a while you may find a new position for your old boss. And that will open up that spot back at your old company! With your background, additional experience, and inside knowledge of the industry, you're a shoo-in for the job!

Don't laugh. It's been known to happen.

SUMMARY

- When change is inevitable, how skillfully you manage those changes will have a lasting impact on the rest of your career and reputation.

- Take care of all your relationships, even the ones you think are safely relegated to your past.
- Whether you have three months, six months, or a year to plan your transition, you can make excellent use of that time if you plan for the change and growth you desire.
- Be a good citizen of your profession. Do what you can to help others along the way.

INTERVIEW

Debra Engel

Former Senior Vice President, Human Resources (retired), 3Com Corporation

DEBRA ENGEL FIRST BECAME *aware of the concept of human resources during a summer job at a Procter and Gamble plant packaging toothpaste tubes into little boxes. She was surrounded by people doing repetitive, tedious work but actually enjoying themselves. She realized that there must be someone who was responsible for making the corporate decisions that would result in the experience employees had on the job. And she knew that she wanted that role, whatever it was.*

That decision would lead to a series of life choices that would ultimately bring her to Silicon Valley, where she worked in HR for Hewlett-Packard, but not for long. Word got out that she was talented, and in 1983 a start-up networking company, 3Com, would successfully recruit her to launch and run its HR department. Attracted to the excitement of building a great company from the ground up, Debra made the risky move (during a pre-boom era when it was practically unheard of to take such an entrepreneurial chance). And in the next fifteen years, she grew the company from eighty employees to 15,000 located all over the world.

At forty-six she was able to "retire" from 3Com. In this interview she talks about the new ways HR careerists can move beyond the traditional definitions of HR and contribute their energies and business acumen to organizations large and small (for profit and nonprofit, as well), helping them make decisions that will benefit the well-being of ever greater numbers of people.

What is the best piece of advice you ever received?

The most important advice my parents gave me was about ambition. For my parents the greatest accomplishment in life is to be a good person. It isn't about making more money, having a bigger house, being known by more people, or working at a higher level. It is about focusing on what kind of work you want to do to have the greatest positive impact. That advice was so freeing because it allowed me to focus on what's *important*, as opposed to symbols of what other people consider to be success. Embracing this advice allowed me to focus on what kind of work I wanted to do, instead of what position I wanted to attain.

Early in my career I received another piece of advice that changed the way I related to people. A boss told me I made people feel stupid. I was so devastated, I cried. All that time I had been working so hard to please people. I thought I had to have all the answers. In the process, I ended up being demeaning to the people who posed the questions. If you flip off the answer before people have had the chance to lay out their angst or describe completely the dilemma or something they've been wrestling with for weeks, it makes them feel stupid. So the advice he gave me was to hold off giving people any answers for twenty-four hours. Say something understanding and supportive when they're in front of you. Make sure you tell them you understand what their issues are, and then tell them you'll get back to them.

It was a miracle. I listened differently. I understood more about the dilemmas that were presented to me. Many dilemmas aren't about the answer. Some are about how you *act* on that answer, how you go from point A to point B. It's about being supportive. It's about how what you do can support the self-esteem of others. There is so much more to any issue that's presented to you than the simple answer to the question.

What is the worst thing new entrants can do as they develop their profession?

Don't live to please your boss. This doesn't mean to be obstinate or adversarial. You just have to have a set of principles by which you live and a point of view. Yes, you need to understand your boss and manage the relationship carefully. But I see so many people lose themselves in that process of just pleasing that they are not unique entities anymore, and they don't have unique contributions to make. You were hired to bring something unique and special and to complement your boss, not mimic him or her.

What is the best thing that they can do?

Know yourself. Know who you are. Be responsible for your own behavior. It's the one set of behaviors you can control, especially in HR when you're feeling whipped around by others in the organization. It's so easy to say, "It's everyone else's fault; they treat HR unfairly." Say instead: "I can control my behavior. What is it about my behavior that I can change to make this situation work?"

Be a lifelong learner. Nothing stands still, especially in these times. If you rest on your laurels, you'll soon be outdated. Your own expertise is dependent on your constant assessment of where you are in your development and what you can do to take yourself to the next step.

It's so important to understand where you are in relationship to the work you want to accomplish. Seek feedback from a variety of people. I know it's hard to do, but put yourself out there and ask others what they think of you in a nondefensive way. If you get the same theme from a variety of people, it's safe to assume that it's probably something you need to change and likely within your power to change.

What risk did you take in your career that paid off for you?

I was too naïve to understand that it was risky at the time, but leaving my position as corporate staffing manager at Hewlett-Packard to help launch 3Com was definitely a risky thing to do. This was in the early 1980s when people didn't job hop much. They certainly didn't leave Hewlett-Packard if they were doing well there. But leaving the big company to go to a little one gave me an incredible education. It was the best of all worlds.

I would recommend to anyone who is in a big company to have a small company experience. When you're in a company of only eighty people, and you're one of the top executives, you are running that company. Small companies have every element that a big company has, except scale. When you're small, what you need to get done doesn't get delegated out to the marketing department or to the engineering department or the sales department.

You have to be making those key decisions along with your colleagues in that boardroom. *You're* studying competitors. *You're* studying financing. *You're* creating the strategy. What an education. What a gift. With large companies, even if you're the top HR person, you may never really see how the company runs.

You mentioned that it was the work, not the *position,* that held the most meaning for you. What was it about the HR career that told you that that is where you would be able to find the meaning you were looking for in your work?

My career aspirations were never around a profession. They were always around work that I wanted to do. Since my post-college years, I've always been intrigued about people in community and the question, "How can people do really good work in a way that they can enjoy it and grow from it?"

After I graduated from college, I went to Procter and Gamble to work on the production line because I had to save money for graduate school. I was struck by the environment they created and how much better it was than when I was a waitress, when I sold magazines over the phone, worked in the grocery store, or did flower arranging. I was so impressed by how efficiently things were run and how happy the people were. And I started asking myself, why were they happy? Does someone think about that or did it happen by accident?

So I went to the personnel manager there. And I asked him, "Who was responsible for this?" Did someone actually sit down and think about this? He said he did it. That was probably somewhat inaccurate, but I believed him, and so I decided right then and there I wanted to be in personnel. Is that cool or what? You can create a place that makes all this stuff, that makes a lot of money, and where people really like doing their jobs. I thought that this was a huge contribution to society. People could go to work. Be happy. Enjoy themselves. Contribute. And take care of themselves.

Over time I discovered it wasn't just about HR. I could be the CEO and do that. I could be a line manager and do that. I could be on boards and do that. In each case, I'm hoping that some piece of what I do is going to make this entire organization and everyone in it better. That's the ambition. So I'm always looking for leverage. What is the way I can leverage myself more than I did last year? How can I impact even more people positively?

With all this ability to make a positive impact on people within organizations—or community, as you put it—how did you prepare yourself for the eventuality of retiring, but still contributing to society?

I started building bridges when I knew I would be leaving within a few years. This was to make sure that I still had a role and relevance after I lost my corporate title. I got an advance taste of what can happen when you lose your title when I went from Hewlett-Packard to 3Com. When I was at HP I had HP's name behind me, and I could call anyone and get my calls returned, just like that. But when I went to 3Com, even in the role of vice president, no one had heard of 3Com. And I couldn't get any of my calls returned. So I knew from that experience how important it is to have connections, a network, in place well in advance of my departure from 3Com.

There was a point in my career when I asked myself: "How can I become a better business leader?" That's when I started thinking about joining boards. Becoming a board member is a different way of viewing the corporation, and it broadens your perspective. But I didn't start out as a board member. My first role was more of an *advisor* to a company.

One of our institutional investors ran HR networking sessions, which I really enjoyed because I'm a big networker. As they had new companies to cultivate, I was one of the people they would refer to give advice. They expected you to advise on HR, but when they discover you have more potential or a broader perspective, and they say, "I'd like to have you on the board. Could you join our board?" I started gravitating quickly toward small entrepreneurial company boards. I have seven or eight of them now.

Once people learn you've served on boards, they start to see you that way. And eventually you move beyond HR. Many of the boards I'm on now don't know I was ever in HR. They don't ask anymore. I'm known as the person who helps them grow the company people-wise. They don't ask me what my background is. Personally, I feel that I'm doing the exact same job I have done for years as an HR person. They just don't call it HR any more.

At this level, it's now called *strategic planning* or *organizational effectiveness*. But the essential HR questions haven't changed. How do you get your team aligned? How do you choose excellent people? What level executive do we need? How do we prepare for the next stage of growth? When do I know that the people I have aren't equipped for that next stage of growth? How do I have that conversation? It's all HR work.

I also was able to bring that skill back to work. It was all part of my personal development. And it became a way to give me a meaningful role to play once I was outside of 3Com.

INTERVIEW

Eva Sage-Gavin

Executive Vice President, Human Resources, Gap, Inc.

AS EXECUTIVE VICE PRESIDENT, Human Resources, of Gap, Inc., Eva Sage-Gavin runs the people function of a company with 165,000 employees and one of the most recognizable American brands worldwide. Eva knew from the time she was fifteen that corporate human resource management held the most promise to her for a fulfilling life's work. And then she set about mapping her career step by step, choice by choice, beginning with a bachelor's degree in industrial and labor relations from Cornell University.

Each item on her résumé reflects a careful decision geared to helping her achieve the topmost HR seat inside a major corporation by the time she was in her forties. And so her career has taken her to such varied companies as PepsiCo, Xerox, Disney Consumer Products, and Sun Microsystems.

One important lesson she came across repeatedly along the way is that "up is not the only way." And sometimes an even better opportunity would come quickly at the heels of a disappointment. In this interview she talks about the importance of planning your career with as much strategy as possible, all the while understanding that surprises—even the unpleasant ones—can propel you further and faster than you could ever have foreseen.

What was the best advice you ever received?

It was actually advice that came in the form of a question when I was making a difficult decision about a possible opportunity: "Do you want your career to be a spider web or a ladder?" Spider webs have all these connecting points going in many different directions, which both strengthen it and make it more functional—and only a relative few of them go *up*. The point as it was presented to me was that by having a lot of lateral experiences in my portfolio that I can draw on, I'd be able to use that diversity of experience throughout my entire career to give me a kind of credibility that I wouldn't have been able to get if I just aimed for upward progression.

This advice came three years into my career when I was disappointed about not getting a promotion, and I found myself making a lateral move. The senior executive who posed the question told me that variety was more valuable in the long run than the upward career climb, and said, "It seems hard to believe this so early in your career, but twenty or thirty years from now you'll cherish some of these moves, and you'll be better prepared as a result." It was hard to hear then, and continued to be hard to hear at other times in my career. But he was right.

Over the years, I did some lateral moves that, in some cases, might have been perceived as downgrades. I went from senior vice president at Disney to vice president at Sun Microsystems, and then back up to senior vice president at Sun. The title wasn't the driver. Getting the experience was. I had gone to Disney after seven and a half years at PepsiCo to get global experience, not to get the title. And before that I went to PepsiCo after ten and a half years at Xerox to get labor experience. It's the variety of experiences that has been the driver of change for me. Not the titles.

Some people might say, "You didn't have to take those risks. You didn't have to make those moves. Who said you needed labor?" In a lot of environments you don't. But why would I want to be locked into one company or one industry when I could build the diversity of experience early in my career when the risks were lower?

The other thing I did to build my spider-web career was to relocate fourteen times. Not only do I have diversity of industries and a diversity of experiences, but I can also establish rapport with just about anyone across multiple industries and globally.

Now I'm at my fifth major corporation in twenty-three years. The experience I've developed in a multi-industry, global, multi-brand career has given me the diversity of skills that have served me well in some tough spots where I have had to make some quick decisions—and the only knowledge I can rely on is my cumulative life experiences.

Having said that, I wouldn't recommend that *everyone* move fourteen times. To be honest, there were a couple of those moves that I probably should have skipped.

What was the moment when your career changed forever?

There were a couple of times in my career when I was really disappointed not being selected for key roles I felt I was ready for. At the time, each event was crushingly disappointing. But amazingly enough, each disappointment opened the way for other amazing things to happen, to the point where I was able to say, "Thank goodness I didn't get that promotion or job."

Each one of those disappointments caused me to take an alternative path that ultimately resulted in a radical change instead of incremental change. I'm so much better off as a result. It made me confident that good things will happen eventually; you have to have a more open set of expectations.

It also made me realize that we make our own luck. You have to be open to unexpected possibilities; you also have to be *prepared* for them. I'm a little more casual about progression and momentum and a lot more relaxed about timeframes than I used to be. But what I'm *not* relaxed about is being really clear about what I'm good at and what I'm not good at. And when I see a hole in my skills, I try to close it as best I can.

If I could advise someone going forward, I'd say: Take risks now, when you can best afford to. When you're beginning, it feels like it's the worst time to take risks. When you're junior, every year seems so important. Every dollar variance between you and others seems so significant. If you can just stay focused on the big picture, it can all work out. But if you get hung up on the exact points in time you expect to have accomplished certain goals, you can get distracted and lose your confidence.

What is the one thing you wish you had done differently?

I never finished my MBA. At this level, working with a board of directors and with CEOs and CFOs of other companies, having a really strong understanding of financial issues would be an incredible value add. If I could go back and do it again, I would finish the MBA and maybe take another run at a line operating role.

The broader your business base can be, the more effective you can be at top levels, understanding the broad underlying principles for creating shareholder value. If you can really nail those early in your career, it's a true advantage. The more grounded you can be early in your career in these areas the better.

Maybe someday, when I have more time, I'll go back to school and learn for the pure love of learning. I might be the seventy-year-old woman in the class getting her degree. Being a lifelong learner is really important to me.

What is the best piece of career advice you have to offer those on the way up?

I keep coming back to the same themes: Build diversity of experiences (both in your career and life) and a broad global knowledge set. Do as much as you can, as fast as you can. Don't lock down too early in terms of deciding that you're only going to be an expert in this or an expert in that. Sample things. Even if you don't do well at something, you can use that experience later to create a bond with someone who is working for you and has that responsibility.

Be open to new experiences. It doesn't necessarily mean you have to change companies. A lot of times it doesn't even mean you have to change jobs. You just have to open your lens to what you think your role is and sign yourself up for task forces and project teams. Sign yourself up for unsolvable problems and solve them anyway. Make yourself invaluable.

What do up-and-coming professionals need to know now that you didn't need to know when you were first starting out?

They need to have a good grounding in organization development and effectiveness, change management, and financial analysis and fundamentals. Fortunately, I had a relatively good grounding coming out of Cornell University, and I use a large percentage of those skills every single day.

I'd also like to suggest that they frequently ask themselves, "Am I living the life I want to live in this exact moment?" Don't wait for that proverbial day when something mysterious will happen to tell you that now is the time to do what you want to do. That day is now. I think September 11 has changed us all forever. Remember, almost all of the people who died that morning were on the job or traveling because of work. If this were the last day you were living, are you spending it the way that holds the most meaning for you? Did you give something? Did you learn something? How is what you're doing benefiting others on a larger social scale? Does your career reflect your larger values and sense of purpose in life?

Last summer I faced a false medical test that said I potentially had a few months to live. I sat down with my family, and we asked ourselves, "What should we do? Should we go on a cruise or a big trip?" But when it came right down to it, I realized that I'm living the life I've always wanted to live. I wouldn't want to change anything else. My husband said, "Yeah, I've always thought that about you."

The only things I wanted to do was to spend more time with my daughter and husband and have more quality time with my close friends. And throw a really big party and wear a red dress. That was it.

I'd been around the world. I've had personal success. I have a great life partner. I'm a mom. And I have a job I really love. The only thing I was missing was the luxury of a little more time. There was nothing else that mattered to me, other than meaningful relationships and spending a little more time with the people I love.

It was a gift to be faced with this crisis. All these adversities ended up to be gifts in disguise, although at the time you could never have convinced me of that.

Now I live my life with a little more courage and high-risk orientation. Once you've been told you're going to die, there's not much else that's going to bug you. I'm blessed with work.

I'd also like to tell up-and-comers in HR to get lots of exposure to different aspects of a business early in their careers. About five years into my career, I left human resources altogether to take a field sales job for two years in the office products division of Xerox. It was the best thing I ever did. I got to work on a commission plan I had designed the year before as a sales analyst. Talk about living in the real world! I got to see how the *intent* of the design compared to what the *reality* of it was. It was not only a great practical experience, it also helped me understand what sales reps go through and what it's like to be turned down ten times in one day by customers. I go back to that experience over and over again and really empathize with what we ask people to do every day.

What's the worst thing they can do to themselves?

Limit their thinking. They should push themselves into acquiring new skills and develop their sense of who they are as broadly as they possibly can. I see people many, many years into their careers who are stuck because they've reached a certain pay and salary level or job title and can't break out of that position to give themselves a different set of experiences or skills, even if they will enhance their future in the long run.

They shouldn't equate success with perfection. You don't have to be perfect. And there may be times when they can't be perfect, no matter how hard they try. I have advised several people over the years, "Pick up your ball and leave that field. Find a field where you're going to be successful." Sometimes the culture that's there is not going to be the right match for you. Don't die trying. Know when to give up and move on. Don't think you have to tolerate unhappiness because you think no one else will appreciate or value you or that you have to make it right somehow where you are before you deserve to go elsewhere. Sometimes it's just not a good fit. Know when to move on.

What characteristics and qualities do you look for when hiring HR professionals today?

I look for business orientation. Are they generally knowledgeable about business? Are they up-to-date with key current events? Have they studied the company and industry that they're coming to talk to you about? Have they asked themselves how they might be able to add value to the specific challenges my department or company is facing?

It's also critical that they have strong consulting skills. I look for big-systems thinkers, people who look for the deeper meaning or issue that lie behind the presenting problem. Even at junior levels, you don't have to always have the answers, but you can still demonstrate your potential by the quality of questions that you ask.

What was the biggest risk you've taken in your career that paid off?

The sales job at Xerox was the biggest risk, and it was the best thing I ever did, no question. I was very effectively mentored throughout those two years. And I then went on to become HR director to the sales group that I had some exposure to. So it was a beautiful blending of credible sales experience with a team that knew I could perform, as well as having the HR functional skill set. I was gone just long enough to pick up some skills, but not gone so long that I fell out of touch with HR.

I was trained in the Xerox sales model called SPIN, which stands for: Situation, Problem, Implication, and Needs. I use that model even now to get to the root cause in an issue. In systems selling, you're not trying to sell a box or a piece of software. What you're really saying is "What is the solution the customer's looking for?"

4

"HEY, I KNOW SOMEONE . . ."

How to Make the Market Come to You

The best job opportunities are rarely published. They are shared in the "hidden" marketplace, passed along quietly from person to person, from search committee to executive recruiter. The only way to tap into this stream of career-building job possibilities is to develop your network of relationships with people who trust you and respect your professionalism. This chapter tells you how to use your HR-specific communities of colleagues and peers to build the career and life you want.

IF YOU'VE BEEN in HR for any amount of time, I'm sure you're familiar with those dreary stacks of résumés, every single one of them piping the refrain "pick me, pick me, pick me." As urgently as you might need to fill that open position, the prospect of slogging through the pitiful pile is about as enchanting as grading term papers. How long can you sustain the hope that somewhere buried in that heap lies even the faintest glimmer of potential?

You know that feeling firsthand. So you are in the best possible position of completely understanding how important it is that, in your own job search and career-building process, you stand out from the crowd from the very beginning. And that résumé? If you manage your own market right, that's still a valuable document, but only to provide necessary data for recruiters and search committees who have already spotted you and want to know more. Don't use your résumé to open doors, unless you love the sound of "pick me, pick me, pick me."

In Chapter 2, I talked about the importance of building a story going forward—how to understand what decisions to make to help you achieve your goals in three- to five-year increments, ultimately to achieve your life's career ambitions. Along the way, you build a different kind of story—a story about who you are, what you represent in terms of values, talent, work ethic, and so forth. In the late 1990s it was popular to talk about personal branding in business, and the principles are still very much the same going forward into the 21st Century. When people hire you, they're not only retaining someone to get the job done but they're also buying the experience they expect you to have. These are all sorts of intangibles that no résumé can really capture, measure, and list on a page or two. These are the qualities of who you are, how people feel about working with you, how people feel about *themselves* when they work with you (which is becoming increasingly important as HR takes the lead in helping companies develop an intentional workplace culture), and what they can count on and trust you to deliver no matter what the external circumstances might be.

This is your reputation—your most powerful career-building tool. It goes where no résumé can go. And it brings back to you an open flow of very intriguing opportunities from people and companies who want to hire someone *just like you.*

If you're thinking, "I'm still in school; I haven't done anything yet to build a reputation," don't kid yourself. People have been talking about you since before you were born, so even from Day One you've had a reputation. Your parents know people who know people who know people. So even if you decide to move cross-country before starting your career, you can leverage the contacts you already have to give yourself a good start. It might not seem like a significant opportunity at the moment, but you never know where it will take you. When I moved to California from my small Pennsylvania hometown, for instance, the first job I landed was courtesy of the oldest son of my family's next-door neighbors, who had relocated to California more than a decade earlier. It changed my whole life.

So no matter where you are in your career, you have already started building your brand. The real issue is how you make the most of it moving forward. And it will be that brand that makes recruiters and hiring managers seek you out, offering you opportunities before you even think that maybe it's time to start looking again.

The view from the recruiter's desk: The value of reputation and relationships is so well-known these days—especially among HR professionals—

that you might be tempted to say to yourself at this point, "Yes, yes, tell me something I don't know." Here's a little something: The most elite positions are filled either by word of mouth or sent to the best search consultants to fill. My office never advertises or posts positions anywhere. We seek out only the best candidates—and we know the best candidates come to us through referrals from people we know. If you're not getting enough calls from the A Player-retained search firms in your area—or the nation—presenting appropriate opportunities that are worthy of your consideration, this chapter will give you valuable ideas for strengthening your network and improving your visibility!

YOUR CIRCLES OF INFLUENCE

Whether you are just starting out or have progressed in your career for a few years, you have probably read a couple of articles or books on networking that encourage you to make a list of everyone you know—usually in categories of your various activities in life. And then what are you supposed to do with those lists? Call these people up and say, "Hey! I'm looking for a job. Let me know if you hear of anything, will you?" That's not much more effective than sending résumés (along with thousands of other people) to posted job openings.

If you need to find a job immediately, by all means, use every avenue, every contact, any scheme you can to get in front of hiring managers. If you need that job, let nothing hold you back. But once you're settled in a position and can buy yourself a little time to review this matter of relationships, reputation, and word of mouth more thoughtfully, return to this book. Remember, this book is about building a successful HR career *over time,* one that progresses logically and gradually, making great use of all your assets as you grow along the way.

Identifying Your Circles of Influence

To start with, we need to organize our thoughts by taking a careful look at the various circles of influence that are in your life right now and that, if you plan well, will be in your career through your working years. You'll see that each circle progresses farther and farther away from your immediate family, social, and work circles. (See Figure 4.1.)

You might be tempted to assume that the outer circle is available to you only as your career progresses and you become more senior. Put that assumption aside for just a few minutes. Let's look at each circle.

Figure 4.1. Circles of Influence.

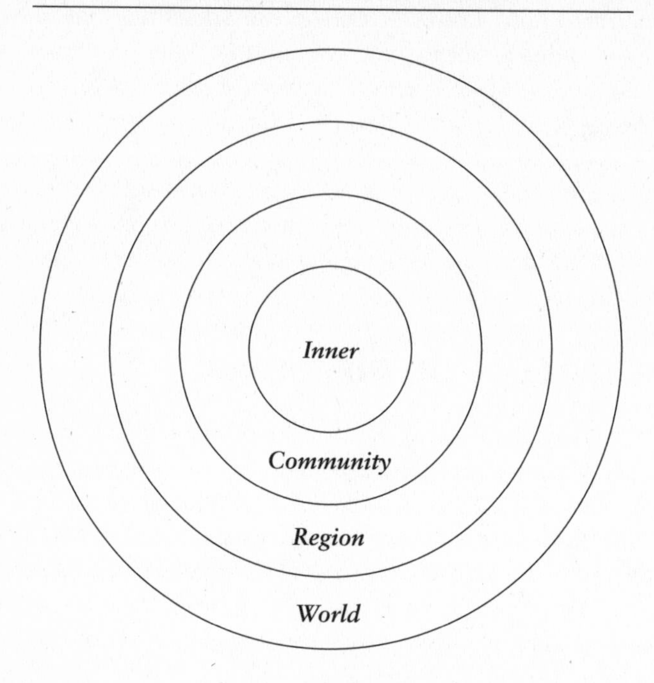

YOUR INNER CIRCLE. This is the circle closest to "home" for you: Your family, your friends, your co-workers, your classmates, and fellow sorority or fraternity members. It can also encompass the people you know through your spiritual community, even the friends of your parents—or the parents of your friends. Because this particular group requires little history, or background, or track record, it's natural for the newest professionals to assume this is primarily their domain. However, remember this chapter is about building word of mouth over time, and therefore even the most senior executives must remember to embrace the people they know in this circle. They probably would not get their next job through this population. But it's entirely possible they can help their contacts in their inner circle begin *their* careers. And since the HR profession depends on 360-degree word of mouth more, probably, than any other profession, it's important that you are known for the many times you've given others a chance to break into the careers of *their* dreams. And a note to the new HR careerists who think that their inner circle can help them: Don't forget that you're in someone else's inner circle. As an HR professional—even a fresh graduate—you are in a privileged position of knowing what jobs are available out there. A word from you can help open doors to your qualified friends. And you will begin building your reputation as someone who brings others through the door you opened for yourself.

YOUR COMMUNITY CIRCLE. This circle contains your colleagues and peers in your town or city, as well as the people you come to know in your HR associations. This circle might also include vendors and consultants (as well as headhunters) you become friendly with, anyone who is in the position of knowing what's going on in your immediate neighborhood. Even the sandwich guy at the local lunch counter might have overheard a tip that could come in very handy to you one day. Members of this circle may include the other parents in your children's school. They may be members of your local chamber of commerce or trade council. You may not see the people in your community circle every day or even every week. But because you're likely to see them regularly, they have a chance to form an opinion about you, just as you have about them. You may not be around when it happens (you may not even *ask* for it to happen), but a little friendly word from one of them in the right ear could cause your phone to ring. Again, don't forget to look for opportunities to make *their* phones ring.

YOUR REGIONAL CIRCLE. As we move farther out in the field of circles, opportunities to get to know and be known beyond your immediate groups increase tremendously. SHRM, for example, has state councils and regional representatives who meet and serve SHRM members in multiple states. Volunteering on committees for the annual regional meetings, for instance, puts you in front of your peers and recruiters from important employers three states over from yours. Likewise, companies of similar size to yours or in similar industries get together on a regional basis to discuss economic or industry issues. There are also federal and state legislative groups that often look for industry representatives to serve on committees, panels, and councils.

YOUR WORLD CIRCLE. The world is your playing field. As you become increasingly comfortable (notice I didn't say *senior*) in your various communities, you can take your influence to settings where the stakes are higher and the field of vision stretches beyond your immediate horizons. Make sure you're an active member of the national levels of your HR professional groups, for instance. Look for opportunities to participate in and volunteer for special committees that are part of your major national associations. Submit articles, case studies, or white papers to the associations' libraries. And, especially if you're passionate about a particular industry, become a member of those related associations. If they have a professional emphasis group (PEG) on human resource management, join it! If they don't, start one.

You can even affect the world of your profession right where you live. If your community or region has a major convention center, the world comes to your door as well. Even if there are no immediate plans for the HR groups to hold their annual conferences there, you can still help influence the business communities that come to your area. The local convention and visitor's bureau (CVB) publishes calendars of scheduled meetings, often several years in advance. Request a copy of that schedule and look for groups that appeal to you. Join them and then volunteer your time and energies to help make their meeting a success. While you're at it, see what volunteer opportunities might be available with the CVB itself. There might be ways you can convene a special assembly of HR leaders in the area who would be available to give concurrent sessions at the conferences.

And, of course, don't overlook the global reach of the Internet. You can make friends far and wide, and influence people's careers and HR practices right there in your home, at your keyboard in the middle of the night.

If you look closely at all these circles of influence, you'll see that there is no real barrier to any of them other than your own vision and ambition for yourself (and, of course, the time you want to take out of your life's other activities to invest in growing your professional stature and reputation). All of these circles will welcome your presence and participation in some way, regardless of how senior you are in your career. There's an appropriate place for you, whether it's on your block or on the world stage.

•

Building Relationships That Make a Difference

The most important thing you can do in your career is to build strong relationships. And one of the most important relationships to build will be the one you have with the chief executive officer (CEO) or other business leaders whom you support. These are the people from whom you can learn the most and can gain the broad perspective you need to move up the career ladder. The executives above your level will be most likely to facilitate your career growth and success—or not—depending on how well you manage those relationships. They have the greatest ability to influence decisions within your company and to make introductions for you to other

CEOs and business leaders in other companies. Essentials for building strong relationships at the executive level include:

- Earn trust and confidence by protecting the confidences of others.
- Learn what business issues keep them awake at night and find ways to help alleviate problems along the way.
- When presenting your leadership team with a problem for their attention, be sure to bring an array of possible solutions they can consider as well.
- Take risks appropriately by presenting opposing views professionally, even if it means that you put your job on the line.
- Show strength by holding your position on important issues; they will respect you for your views. However, once a decision is made, support it.
- Carry yourself with self-respect and dignity consistent with the level of professionalism you observe of those several levels above where you are.

•

NOW WHAT?

What you actually do inside those circles, however, can be determined by your stature within your company or your profession. These following activities can be done in any of the circles. They are things that every HR star does to some extent, and they're open to you no matter where you are in your career (even speaking, as you'll see). The only difference is how you do them.

Let's start with *speaking*. If you're brand new to the profession, you might be asking yourself, "What could I possibly speak about?" In *HR from the Heart,* Libby Sartain (now Chief People Officer at Yahoo!) tells the story of how she would go back to her university the years immediately following her graduation and give talks to classes of students coming up behind her. Her topic: Getting their first job and surviving out in the real world for the first several years. No matter who you are and what you've done, there is almost always someone a few steps behind you who can learn from your examples and experiences.

If you're completely new to speaking, joining Toastmaster's is an excellent way to obtain the confidence you need. But you've heard that before. Here's what's new: Don't join the Toastmaster's sponsored inside your organization, if there is one. Go outside your group. Find a Toastmaster's conveniently located in your community's busiest business center. Commute to the nearest big city if you can, for that matter. That way you accomplish three goals (at least): You polish your speaking skills, boost your confidence, and put yourself in new circles of acquaintances—people who can pass your name on to an inquiring recruiter . . . or, don't forget, people whose names *you* can pass on when a recruiter asks you for leads. Maybe not this year, maybe not five years from now. Maybe the fortuitous phone call will happen fifteen years from now. But the contacts you make now will make that call all the more productive. The future is going to happen anyway. Wouldn't it be great to meet it with a well-developed contact list of longtime friends and colleagues who have been developing their careers parallel with yours? Then you can gather at five-star hotels all over the world laughing about the good old days and remembering when.

If you're more senior and seasoned in your career, you are probably well-aware of the importance of being in front of audiences. But if you've been too focused on getting your daily job done, it's possible you'll need this extra reminder. At the very least, because HR is such a dynamic corporate function, changing and maturing all the time, it's your professional obligation to help add to the body of knowledge by sharing what you've learned. Volunteer to participate on panels and concurrent sessions in your community and beyond. The larger consulting firms, for instance, hold annual events showcasing clients and successful projects. These can be great opportunities to make yourself and your accomplishments known across a variety of companies, all of whom identify with you already because you're part of that consultant's select group. You don't have to be a spellbinding motivational speaker, complete with choreographed platform skills. You just have to be clear, impassioned, and informative. Your colleagues (and recruiters in the audience) want to know what you know. They don't care about the song-and-dance flash and performance that comes along with the professional speaking crowd. So don't be shy; just get out there sharing. Whether you're currently looking for a new opportunity or not, your name will get around. And your phone will start ringing and keep ringing.

If you're more junior, volunteer to participate in the orientation meetings of your company's new hires. This is a great way to meet people who will be filling roles all over the company (and up and down the organization chart from you). If you're a relative newcomer to the company yourself, you can relate to these orientation participants on a more contemporary level (even if they're senior to you on the organization chart). You'll always be able to refer to each other as members of the same generation of employees in your company.

Finally, another fabulous way to build visibility is to volunteer to do training in your company—become certified in delivering internal training courses. Many of these programs are developed by external management training companies that provide great "Train-the-Trainer" programs.

Get active in your *trade and professional associations.* Every industry and every profession has an association to support its interests and promote its key causes—especially before local, state, and federal governments. In HR, of course, there is the Society for Human Resource Management (SHRM) and its hundreds of local chapters. There is also the International Personnel Management Association (IPMA), and the American Society for Training and Development (ASTD), among many others directly supporting and promoting HR concerns and interests. You should be active in at least one professional group. In addition, there is a trade association that represents the interests of your company's industry. If you expect to stay in the industry, as well as in the HR profession, it's in your best interest to be a member of that group as well.

However, it's not enough to be just a member. You need to be *active* in the association. That way you emerge from the crowd of faces that show up only once a month for the meetings. Committees are always seeking volunteer help, and almost any activity will help you meet new people, giving them the chance to know you. However, the absolute best committees for truly circulating among your peers and colleagues are the membership, program, and fund-raising committees. With these subgroups, you meet current members, prospective newcomers, and thought leaders who may speak before your monthly meeting. Try to introduce them at your meetings. Every time you stand up in front of the gathered membership, that is a few minutes in the spotlight. Someone will notice.

The public relations committee could also be beneficial to your career in that you stand to develop an ongoing relationship with your local workplace reporters, who may get in the habit of calling you for your considered opinion (and quotes) on major employment issues of your area.

As you progress in both your career and your experiences in the associations, strategize ways to qualify for positions on their boards. Each association has different by-laws, so it's difficult to make blanket recommendations in this book. However, invest the first several years of your participation in learning the inner workings of the association by watching how the leaders make it to the top. Find an especially influential member inside the association's power structure to help put you on that path as well. With the advice and grooming of such a mentor, you'll be given the projects and learning opportunities that will pave your way to higher and higher leadership positions inside the organization. From that vantage point you'll be able to help drive the future of HR in your community (or the future of your industry, if this is a trade association).

With this kind of exposure, you could also find yourself tapped for volunteer positions with even greater visibility inside the economic development engines of your region. The local chamber of commerce, for instance, or the trade council, or a special governor's initiative may seek you out for your contributions as you become a seasoned, recognized participant in making things happen in your world. The old maxim, "If you want something done, ask a busy person," holds true here. The busier you are, the more people will ask of you. The upside of this maxim is, of course, the busier you are the more often your name will come to mind for all sorts of opportunities—even a new career opportunity.

One way of becoming a prominent HR "player" in your community is to *help your company become prominent.* Tell your corporate communications department (with any necessary approvals of your superiors, of course) that you would like to help it put out the good word about what your company is doing. Make a list of the various projects out of HR that put your company in a positive light and describe them to your corporate communications counterpart to explore potential for press releases and the possibilities of local reporters writing features. Volunteer to lead the project by applying to be on any of the various Best Employers lists that are published every year. Tell your public relations representative that you would like to be on the list of employees cleared to speak with the press. Ask to be given media training so that you understand the rules and fine points of giving interviews.

Volunteer to support your company's *governmental affairs* office—especially in its employee-related public policy activities: Immigration law. Parental leave. Privacy laws. Safety regulations. If your company has a governmental affairs office, it is likely to be knee-deep in lobbying on behalf of (or against) pending legislation that could directly impact the workplace. If you are senior enough in the HR department so that it's appropriate for you to speak publicly on the key issues your company is dealing with, by all means volunteer your time and efforts. You may find yourself describing the impacts of new bills before your local Rotary meetings. And eventually you might find yourself at the state capitol or the nation's Capitol speaking in front of a specially convened panel of legislators tasked to study these issues at society's highest levels.

If you're not senior enough right now to be an appropriate spokesperson on these issues, support the HR person who is. Be that person's lieutenant behind the scenes, even if it means photocopying and stapling reams of documents for distribution to the special subcommittees. Be there, get noticed, learn the ropes from within. As you gain the necessary experience, you'll be given the chance to step forward more and more.

Help your company do well by *doing good.* Companies of all sizes have some form of community affairs function. It could be as elaborate as a richly endowed multi-million-dollar foundation, complete with nonprofit status. Or it could be a loosely jointed collection of energetic employees looking for a way to give back to their communities. No matter what the footprint of your company's community affairs activities may be, you can leverage the role your company plays in your community into one that offers high-impact benefits to the recipients of its largesse. Community fund-raisers know that businesses are among the most important sources of operating revenue every year. And as a representative of your company, you can provide a vital link between financial need and ultimate solutions. At the same time, you give yourself the opportunity to meet a caliber of citizens who are passionate about your community's future and the needs of those less fortunate. How active you personally can become in your company's community activities depends, again, on your time and energy. Even the well-established corporate foundations depend on and celebrate the generosity of their employees. So at the very least, you can organize and drive memorable charitable events throughout the years—events that not only support the community, but, through the shared experiences of giving in active ways, bond and engage the employees like no other employee engagement initiative can.

Whether you are active inside or outside the company, find ways to partner with and add value to what's being done already. Don't wait until you think you've been around long enough to be able to contribute something of true value. I've seen the careers of candidates blossom almost completely as a result of who they know and who knows them. They worked hard for that advantage and they deserved it. Absolutely.

If ongoing responsibilities or obligations make you feel overwhelmed just reading those words in this book, start by picking projects with defined end points. Get something accomplished. Have something to point to as having had an important part in making it happen. Have a story to tell. And then find ways to tell it—preferably to large groups.

•

How to Get Published

No matter where you are in your career (even if you haven't started it yet), you have experience, a point of view, an opinion that other people will benefit from reading about. And no matter where you are in your career, *you* will benefit from the effort you invest in getting published. Getting published increases your visibility. People you don't even know will come up to you and say, "I just read your article the other day. Wow, it was really informative and useful!"

Unfortunately, as any professional writer will tell you, getting published isn't always easy. But you can make it much easier for yourself by taking these essential steps to get started:

1. *Consider your publishing options:* The newsletters and websites of your local professional association chapters are always seeking thoughtful insights from their professional members. Contact the committee chairs and brainstorm some of your ideas with them. Be sure to emphasize the point that your perspectives come from real-life experience "in the trenches." National magazines such as *HR Executive, HR Magazine,* and *HR Innovator* welcome articles from practitioners as well. They're significantly harder to get into, though, and you'll increase your chances after you've been published three or four times in other publications. Don't forget the publications and websites serving your company's industry. Their readers deserve to benefit from the HR point of view too!
2. *Collaborate with a favorite consultant:* Consultants are always looking for opportunities to get their own publicity through publishing. If you're working with a consultant on an especially exciting or groundbreaking project, join forces and create an article featuring both perspectives. The consultant may already have the editorial contacts you both need to get the article into print.
3. *Team up with your corporate communications office:* Your company's corporate communications office may welcome your interest in writing for publication. You will be helping them achieve *their* objective of getting exposure for your company. They're experts in working with editors and writing. So they may be very happy to help you write and place articles that will make your company look good.
4. *Don't write alone:* You don't have to be a great writer to be published. You just have to deliver great writing. Find a freelance writer who has a background in HR to help you. Your corporate communications office may have a listing of local freelancers. Or look at the by-lines in the HR-related magazines, which routinely use freelancers. They can help you navigate the unfamiliar territory of publishing.

Getting published takes time and dedication and maybe even a few long hours into the night as you polish up that perfect article. But you'll find that it's well worth the effort as your visibility increases throughout your various circles of influence!

•

HOW TO BREAK INTO COMPLETELY UNKNOWN TERRITORY

The ideas I've just presented assume that you're already ensconced in a company and a community where you will be for a few years. But what if you have in mind a drastic move? Perhaps you want to move three thousand miles away to another part of the country. Or perhaps you have found an industry you love and want to find your way into it. Or perhaps both. Lucky you! How wonderful it is to have a dream. Now you just have to plot your way to it.

As always, your way will be made that much easier if someone on the inside knows you. But at this point, you have no prospects, no introductions. You only have the telephone. And it's up to you to pick it up and make the first effort.

Take heart in knowing that, no matter who you are and where you want to go, there are people on the other end who have something in common with you. And they would probably be very happy to help you achieve your mission. You just have to find out who those people are and introduce yourself. And it's almost as easily done as said.

- *Give yourself plenty of time.* Establishing a reputation and word of mouth takes time, whether you do it locally or long distance. It takes even more time if you try to do it across thousands of miles or across the chasm that separates completely unrelated industries. No matter what drastic change you're trying to accomplish, you'll be most successful if you take the time necessary to do it right.
- *Create a target list of companies or individuals you want to tap into.* Again, this is where memberships in associations and industry trade groups are excellent investments. With the password that comes with your membership, you can go on-line and search the membership directories according to key words, such as company name, title, or location. As long as you're not soliciting business or begging for a job, you are most likely within the

association's membership rules if you contact these people, even out of the blue. Because you're also a member of their association, you already have something important in common with them. And they may be willing to give you a few moments of their time.

- *Think of them as your colleagues and peers.* Just because they are where you want to be, that doesn't mean that they're securely ensconced behind thick walls of achievement. By virtue of your passion and your profession, you're already one of them, especially if you don't want anything from them more valuable than a few minutes of chat and advice.
- *Make it clear to them right away that you are under no pressure to get immediate results.* Try to be relaxed; tell them up-front that you're happy where you are and that you are thinking that within a few years you would like to be where they are—whether it's their geographic location or industry. Be up-front and tell them that you're making initial networking calls. If you are planning to visit their area (as you should be sooner or later), tell them you'd like to meet them in person and perhaps invite them for coffee or lunch to trade ideas. Your main objective at this point is strictly and exclusively to start making friends in their area. Who would say no to that?
- *Don't take rejection personally.* Well, some would say no to that. Some people may interpret your interest in their industry or community as potential competition. And the most competitive of these people may not welcome you. If you get the brush-off, remind yourself that there's at least one in every crowd. And let it go. Since you're not selling anything at the moment, you have nothing at stake. So there's nothing to lose. Move on to the next person on your list. (*Note:* Make sure you have more than one person on that list!)
- *Return the favor.* Make sure you're always available to open doors for others. It may be an opportunity to pay it back or "pay it forward." Either way, remember that you're an important resource to others just as much as you need the resources of others.
- *Improve your chances of a warm reception by positioning yourself in some unique way.* Even if your passion for the industry or the area is the only thing that sets you apart, go with that. But

preferably there is something else that would position you as a fresh, unique new entry in their field. Without that extra little something to set you apart, though, you are more easily dismissed by busy people as yet another "wannabe." One psychotherapist I know of has written seven books and has years of extensive experience coaching and counseling corporate executives of A Player companies. He had it in mind to move from the West Coast to Florida, and so he sent out a few emails to the leadership of association local chapters in the communities that interested him. They were very generic emails introducing himself as a therapist interested in moving to Florida. I wasn't at all surprised to hear that he received standard email back from all his contacts saying that Florida is saturated with therapists and they knew of no openings. In other words: "Buzz off!" Florida may be saturated with generic therapists, but is it saturated with highly respected, published therapists with decades of experience coaching A Player executives? My guess is probably not so much. The therapist should have led with that detail. He might have been just the person his discouraging correspondents were looking for to help *them* emerge from the pack and grow their practices.

- *Call; don't email.* The therapist also made the mistake of emailing these contacts. It's a lot harder to brush off a professional, polite human voice on the phone than to press the delete key on an eager email. Of course, it's best if you are able to drop the name of a mutual acquaintance. But chances are, especially if you're making a big leap in geographic location or industry, you won't have mutual friends. Not yet, at any rate. If you are one of those people who dreads making calls out of the blue, the best I can say here is: Get over it. There's some comfort in knowing that you'll probably get the person's voice mail at least the first time around. So you can break the ice in a recording. It's a start anyway!

- *Be there.* Go to the meetings. Speak at the meetings, for that matter. Local chapters of organizations value an expert perspective from someone who comes from another industry or another part of the country. You'll have a cachet of the exotic about you, and you'll be carefully listened to by a roomful of hundreds of people you need to know! If your plan is to move to an entirely different part of the country, try to time an exploratory visit there with an important annual or semi-annual meeting of your profession or industry. Even if you're not on the agenda, a few good receptions will give you the business cards you need—and the firsthand acquaintances—to be able to make that follow-up call with confidence.

NOW THAT YOU HAVE A REPUTATION, WHAT DOES IT SAY ABOUT YOU?

It's one thing to have a reputation. It's an entirely different thing to have a *wonderful* reputation. Later in this book I talk about what it means to be 100-percent referenceable. But for the time being, think about the people you know and what they would have to say about you should a recruiter or search committee member inquire.

How would the people who work with you (or used to work with you) describe your ethics and principles? One absolutely brilliant candidate was sunk because an employee of the hiring company used to work with him years before. She found out he was on the short list for consideration, and she told a key decision maker, "He's wonderful, he's talented, he's hard-working. But I couldn't work for him again. The last time I felt burned by something he did." That candidate never found out why he wasn't called in for the interview. I wasn't about to tell him and ensnare myself or my client in a potentially litigious situation.

Take care of your relationships as you go along. This isn't always easy because in HR you may find yourself between two functions competing for funds or priority. Overall HR is chartered with influencing its organization to do the right thing. Fair or unfair, it's expected to be the conscience of the company. And that will put you on the spot, especially in a company that emphasizes the power of relationships. When those functions get into a win/lose competition, those relationships will be strained. And you must come out of the struggle looking as impartial and businesslike as possible.

You can minimize the possibility that someone will say about you later that you "burned" them. If you are forced to take sides, *before* you make your position public, take the party on the "losing" side aside and privately explain to him or her the reasoning behind your choice. Honor his or her perspective by acknowledging how difficult it was for you to come to the conclusion that you did finally, and then reassure that person that it wasn't personal and that you will do anything and everything you can to support his or her initiatives in the future. Good business principles will tell you that even when you are forced to disappoint a customer, you must do everything you can to make sure that the customer feels at least well taken care of and respected. You should think of the businesspeople you work with as customers you don't want to disappoint. That way *you* won't get burned years later by the residual bad feelings harbored by a co-worker who remembers the time when you didn't support him or her at a time when it really counted.

You also want your reputation to say that you pick your battles wisely and well. The bromide that says that the only bad press is no press at all is wrong, wrong, wrong! Getting bad press in HR is a very bad thing. I once worked for a wonderful, talented HR leader who was known for being ethical and honest. Eventually he went to work for a foreign-owned company with substantial operations in the United States that refused to abide by U.S. nondiscrimination laws. He tried valiantly from within to influence a change, but he failed. Motivated by strong feelings of taking a stand for what's right, he sued the company for discrimination. The story bounced around the press and the courts for years and years. And eventually there was some kind of undisclosed settlement. Unfortunately, it wasn't enough to keep him financially secure for the rest of his life. He was never able to pick up his career where he left off. And, as I heard it, this wonderful, smart, talented, and dedicated HR professional died homeless.

If you're going to take a stand of massive proportions, think about the career implications of your action. In this case, it probably wasn't a fight worth fighting. It probably didn't change a thing inside the company, and his career was destroyed. And the corporate world lost a wonderful HR visionary who still had so much to give. But what company would want to hire someone who has a record of suing his employer? True, technically speaking, he was morally right. And yes, in the United States we have laws protecting whistle-blowers from retribution. But we have no laws forcing future employers to take a chance on these people. And why should they when they have a selection of wonderfully qualified candidates who have more docile résumés?

On the other hand, because HR is considered the moral compass of the company, as a recruiter I will instantly discard candidates who have any story of dishonest or unethical behavior attached to their reputations. Just as in the example above, why should I present these people when I have a selection of wonderfully qualified candidates who have spotless records? If you have some moments in your past that you deeply regret and wish you could relive so you can do them differently, the chances are excellent that you can prevail over them—especially with the passage of time or a cross-country relocation. But the hard truth is that you will most likely be on your own in this objective. Most recruiters will pass you up, primarily because they have drawers full of résumés they can present without apology.

Have you ever noticed that many people who are motivated to go to networking events are people who are eager to get job or business leads? Networking should never be an *event.* It should be part of your way of life. Reputations and relationships are built over time. Word of mouth happens gradually. It can be the most positive, powerful process in building your life's work. And as people come to know you, throughout all your circles of influence, they'll be coming to you to see if you happen to know of anyone who meets their needs. And you can be sure that you will be at the top of minds when others come to them with the same question. Work those circles throughout your entire life and career—not just when you're on the hunt for your next job.

SUMMARY

- The most successful leadership-bound HR professionals will tell you that many of their opportunities came from their expansive network of friends and colleagues.
- You can be completely new to the profession and still have access to many of the same networking opportunities that your senior colleagues enjoy.
- One of the best ways to gain visibility is to help your company and co-workers achieve their success.
- Take care of your reputation as diligently as you take care of your career. Decide what it is you want to be known and respected for, and make sure your behavior and choices are always compatible with the person you want to be.

INTERVIEW

Mary McLeod

Executive Vice President, Human Resources, Charles Schwab & Co.

BEGINNING HER ADULT *working life as a dental hygienist, Mary McLeod made her leap into the corporate world by casually answering a newspaper ad for a trainer for Andersen Consulting (now Accenture). Her potential was immediately noticed, and her regular promotions and assignments soon led her to the opportunity of opening the Washington, DC-based Change Management Services, a new Andersen venture. She also held HR vice president positions in two of GE Capital's largest businesses, as well as being senior vice president, HR, for Hallmark Entertainment after having put in some time as international HR director for Hallmark Cards. Before joining Schwab, she would invest part of her career in the high-tech world of Cisco Systems, where she was vice president of HR for Cisco's Global Sales Organization and Corporate Business Functions and Global Manufacturing.*

In addition to being executive vice president of HR for the 16,200-employee Charles Schwab & Co., she is also chief of staff to the Office of the CEO and a member of the Executive Committee. In this interview she talks about the importance of being authentic in your everyday dealings, as well as offering senior leadership true added value by bringing to the strategic table essential insight and knowledge they can't get elsewhere.

What is the best piece of advice you have ever received?

One of my clients gave it to me when I was consulting for Andersen, actually. He said, "Tell me something I don't know."

When I think about my career in HR, that's one of the things that has made me successful in working with business leaders. I try to bring fresh new value to every encounter with these people. It's not easy. Corporate CEOs are among the top thinkers in the world. It's really intellectually challenging to give them ideas that they've never thought of.

What is the best advice you have to offer others?

Don't limit yourself early in your career. Try to get as much breadth as possible as fast as possible. The amount of different kinds of experiences you have will differentiate you from others. What you want to be able to say when you go into an interview is, "Of a thousand responsibilities that exist in a job, I've got experience in 999 of them." Everyone wants people who have already "been there and done that" when it comes to the requirements of the open position.

When you consider a candidate for a fast-track HR spot, would you value variety over longevity? How do you perceive job hoppers these days?

It depends on why they've hopped. If they've changed jobs a lot because they've failed consistently, that troubles me. If they've changed jobs because they've been promoted or they've had a lot of opportunities that have provided breadth, I consider that a positive sign.

So if they were able to explain their past in terms of being strategic, that would be to their advantage?

Yes, I would respect that actually. The first question I ask people in an interview is, "What is the most complex work you've ever done?" And the second question is, "What is the most unique work you've ever done?" If they give me good answers to those questions, I don't need to know anything else. In today's business world, everything is about complexity.

What do up-and-comers need now that you didn't need when you first started your career?

They need versatility and experience in the United States and abroad. Globalism is more important now than ever. They need experience working with different cultures, different kinds of scenarios. And they need experience in a whole range of business, not just HR work. It's all about being able to do a variety of things.

What lesson did you learn when you were working abroad that you can continue to use anywhere?

Although it seems overly simplistic, the biggest thing I learned was this: If you go to work in a place and try to be something you're not, you don't do your best work. I'm an American and everyone expects me to be an American. I need to be respectful of their culture and try to fit in. But I don't have to be something I'm not. That attitude has helped me have the confidence to bring all my past experiences to a unique situation in another country and figure out what's right for that particular situation.

What is the best thing new entrants into the HR profession can do for themselves?

I advise people to try to work for a company that is going to have a formal development program for them. General Electric, Pepsi, Johnson & Johnson are examples of companies that will actually invest two years of the company's money in an individual's development. That is a valuable career launching pad for people. Sure, you can certainly get that in smaller companies and start-ups as well. But it's harder because it lacks structure and you have to do it by yourself—which is hard to do if you're new to the profession. You can't know what you need and how to get it. A formal development program early in your career is a big differentiator that will benefit you throughout the rest of your working life. If the company you're going to work for doesn't have a formal development program, then work with your manager to create one that works for you and for the firm. It's worth the up-front time to do that, for both you and the business.

What is the worst thing that new entrants can do *to* themselves?

They shouldn't limit themselves. Early in a career, it's hard to know what you want to do long term, so we're back to the comments that I made earlier about breadth. If you gain experience early in a bunch of different areas, you have a lot of different options as you progress in your career. If you specialize early, and then twenty years later you decide you want to branch out, it's much harder. So until and unless you know what you want to do for the rest of your career, focus on breadth, even if it means you have to do lateral or even backward career moves along the way.

5

RECOVER FROM YOUR MISSTEPS

If you are going to be in HR for any significant length of time, you will likely stumble into a career-damaging misstep or two. Don't let a few fouls and errors throw you out of the game. In this chapter I'll reassure you that there are very few missteps that you truly won't be able to recover from. And you will gain some perspectives and practical advice on how to continue moving forward, even after a misstep when you'd give anything to do things over again.

MISTAKES HAPPEN. Sometimes they're terrible mistakes. But you can recover from just about anything. For instance, one person I know was a staffing director who was alleged to have taken kickbacks from search firms. He was lucky he was just fired. He could have been prosecuted. But he was still out of a job. He licked his wounds for a bit. And then, after enough time passed, he started a business—his own placement firm. And over the years he has built a nice living for himself placing engineers in technology companies for a fee. Over time, many people have either forgotten or forgiven. Although it may not be the career he had envisioned, he has made a good living. He has not, and most likely never will, however, land a significant management position as a staffing or human resources executive. There are some missteps in business that cannot be recovered from, and most of the time they are those related to ethics, honesty, and trust.

There's an expression in Hollywood that is used when a total dog of a film—bad script, bad actors, bad production, an overall hopeless case—turns out to be box-office gold: "No one knows anything." That same expression is used when a charming gem of a picture fails utterly. "No one knows anything."

No one knows anything. And for that reason, never be too quick to condemn your own prospects because there are a few nicks and dings on your résumé. Our careers can last thirty, forty, even more than fifty years if we're lucky. That's a long time to expect anyone to be perfect. In fact, if there aren't some questionable moments or decisions in your past, that alone may be something to worry about. As you progress through your career, you are supposedly rising in the ranks, becoming more vulnerable to the vagaries of business—and expected to take risks. Not all of your risks are going to play out well. It can't be helped.

The first word in your profession is "human," and as humans we're all essentially flawed. We're bound to take a few missteps along the way. But their accumulated effect shouldn't stop us in our tracks, no matter how compounded they may seem to be. There is always a way back into the game. You just have to be more focused about it, perhaps willing to compromise your expectations a bit at first for the sake of getting back on the correct track. The important thing is to stay alert to the signs things aren't going the way you had planned and to make your journey back to your objectives as quickly as possible.

In this chapter, we'll look at the variety of missteps that can trip you up and how you can recover from each one. But before we go into the specific tactics, it's important that we touch on a more personal, more sensitive point. If you feel truly overwhelmed by an indefinable feeling of shame or of having a professional track record that is too flawed to fix, you may want to seek a different kind of counsel before and while you recover your career future. I'm not a psychologist, so I would be presumptuous to go into specific prescriptive steps you can take to recover your sense of joy, self-esteem, and peace of mind. However, it would also be unkind not to mention this particular barrier to your success at this point. Like everyone in the human resources field, we know full well that depression (from mild to serious) is an epidemic in our society. As Wynn Resorts' senior vice president and chief human resources officer, Arte Nathan, says, "It's a thief of time," and no one—no matter how resolute or self-disciplined—is immune from its ravages. Growing your career is stressful enough as it is without laboring under the added weight of despair. Seek the help you need to support your mental health as you move through the process of creating career success in HR.

A misstep is just that—an error that can be corrected with time and a plan. If it feels more weighty than that, reach out for help.

With that said, let's look at some of the common missteps—large and small—that can get in the way of your HR career success:

- *The new job you took turned out to be different from what you expected it to be.* For instance, you were promised that the company is HR-friendly and supports the initiatives of its chief of people. But you quickly discover that the CEO cherishes, say, the research and development (R&D) group even more. The handwriting is on the wall when you're in some kind of power struggle with R&D, and you know you will not be able to get the support you need to be effective.
- *You oversold your skills and discovered afterward that you were unable to deliver.* We all need "stretch" assignments. They help us grow and discover the frontiers of our abilities. You did a great job of selling yourself, but now you realize that the stretch is beyond your grasp. And it's becoming apparent to others as well.
- *You left HR in a boom economy thinking it would be easy to re-enter once your sabbatical in the Costa Rican jungle is over or your new baby has entered preschool.* But a market change reduced the demand for your skill set and experience. This happened to many people in the height of the economic boom of the late 1990s. Thoroughly expecting the demand to be there waiting for them when they got back from wherever they went, they discovered that the search for their next position is taking twelve to eighteen months longer than they had anticipated.
- *You have the reputation of being unwilling or unable to make difficult decisions.* Again, this can be increasingly difficult in a down market. Maybe you have to face laying off hundreds of employees you had personally hired during the growth years. Or you have to change out one executive (who has become a personal friend over the years) with another who is more suited to the challenges of the current market conditions. These are terribly difficult decisions to make, especially in a career that's built on cultivating relationships. But HR is a piece of the overall business, and if you can't make those decisions in a businesslike fashion, you'll be quickly seen as ineffective yourself.

There are more serious missteps that can cause you to stumble in your projected career growth path:

- *Your executive team is charged with fraud, and the employees have lost their retirement.* While your own name might not be listed among the defendants, the question "Where was HR during all this?" is on everyone's lips. Other companies are going to be unwilling to consider candidates with that kind of past. And recruiters are likely to skip over their résumés entirely in favor of candidates they can present with more confidence.

- *Your reputation is dragged through the mud along with the company's.* Similar to the above example, it's possible to be in a well-performing company that has the misfortune of some terrible press. If you stay, your own name is bound to be damaged. If the issue is illegal, unethical, or immoral, and you continue to stay, your company's reputation will be attached to your career, even though you didn't have a direct hand in the problem.
- *You stayed too long in one company.* If you continue to grow the entire time, it doesn't necessarily have to be a negative factor. But if you pulled a Rip Van Winkle, put your head down for a moment, only to look up seventeen years later and wonder where the time flew, you will be a difficult sell to a search committee.
- *You have a history of job hopping.* Anyone can make a mistake in a job selection and have a short stint as a result. Job hopping becomes a detriment when you have three, four, or five one-year jobs in different companies. Then it begins to look like the problem is you.
- *You went down with the sinking ship.* When you're so invested in a company and its long-term success, it's hard to grasp the fact that it has suddenly started going down—maybe through no fault of its own or your own. Loyalty is nice, but it may not always be career-enhancing. And at some point you must decide to cut your losses. Hiring authorities are attracted to people with success stories. When you are in the job market during your company's uptic, you can tell the story of its success. Don't wait too long or you will have to tell the story of the company's decline.
- *You moved to another function within the company and then decided you'd like to return to HR.* In most companies that have a culture of valuing executives who are willing to experience other pieces of the business, this could actually be a benefit to your career. However, if you move to a non-HR-related function and stay there for, say, five years, it's going to be harder to convince hiring executives that your heart truly is in HR. Recruiters and hiring managers will be asking themselves: Why did that per-

son leave? Why does he want to come back now? Does he really want to be in HR, or is this a fall-back position because his fancy marketing job was eliminated? If you aspire to be vice president of HR one day, it's good to explore other areas of the business. But keep those assignments short—one or two years at the most.

- *You stayed too long in a specialty area.* If you stay ten years or more in a single HR specialty, you may become pigeon-holed in that specialty. It will be difficult to disconnect yourself from that specialty role, especially in the eyes of the relative short-timers cycling their way through your department. You were there when they arrived; you were there when they left. In addition, it becomes impractical to jump to another function after you've invested so many years in one specialty. By that time you are likely to be at the top of the pay grade for that function, and how likely is it that you are going to be attractive to another function at that same pay level? If they're going to spend that kind of money, they can get someone who actually has experience in that particular specialty.
- *You neglected you.* You invested so much time and energy in your job, you neglected the rest of your life. Do you have a personal life? Do you know what your kids look like? Have you invested so much for so long that you've lost your passion about what you do? You can work sixty or seventy hours a week to get through a crisis or some major peak, but no one can do it for twenty, thirty, or forty years. Be sure you are taking care of *you* personally, emotionally, and physically. That will add more value long term to your career than burning the midnight oil indefinitely.

So you made a mistake. What are you going to do about it? It depends on the mistake. For every mistake there is at least one solution. I have grouped the above mistakes into eleven major categories and have provided general guidelines for solutions. Take heart. For every way into trouble—real or perceived—there are at least two ways back out.

1. THE WRONG FIT

As an experienced HR professional, you are probably better-equipped than most people to spot a bad fit quickly. But does that mean you move quickly to fix it? Probably yes, provided you make the move strategically and avoid burning bridges.

The good news is that the sooner you make the determination to leave the new job, the less likely it is that your new colleagues will take it personally. But you still have to take action with sensitivity, tact, and some political acumen. It's best to sit down and have a heart-to-heart talk with the person who hired you. There may be some consolation in knowing that, if you're feeling the poor fit, they're probably thinking the same thing as well. If you handle this separation gracefully, maybe you can help them find your replacement. And maybe they can help you find the next job.

If your tenure at this company is short, you need to be able to tell the story about what happened in a way that doesn't put you in a negative light. It would be best to try to agree with your employer on specific wording to explain your short tenure. The truth is always best. You can honestly say, "It just wasn't the right fit." Just be prepared to explain why tactfully.

Or you can stay for a couple of years and make the most of your new opportunity. If you have a few short-tenure jobs on your résumé already, you should do everything you can to make the most of a less-than-optimum situation. Find a way to turn it into a positive experience and see what you can learn from it—new ways of making a silk purse out of the proverbial sow's ear. If the job is substantially less challenging than you were hoping, use that extra time and additional brain bandwidth as an opportunity to brush up on your education or obtain additional training. Or tap into your own superior expertise and provide additional training to your fellow employees to help them grow their prospects. You may feel as though your career has been temporarily marooned on some desolate island for a couple of years, but that doesn't mean you can't make a difference on that island.

If the company has revealed itself to be illegal or unethical, cut your losses. There is no good way to stay. You never want to compromise your own values and sense of honesty. And you don't want your name tarnished by the bad press that is just around the corner. If you're financially strapped and you have no option but to stay, get very aggressive about finding another job and resign the instant you can.

Think twice about whistle-blowing. Although you are legally protected by federal whistle-blower laws, companies are very reluctant to hire whistle-blowers. They're afraid you might blow the whistle on them one day. And for all they know, you might be a crazy person looking for trouble, making things up, seeking publicity. It's a rare company that doesn't have a skeleton or two in its closet, and most situations aren't black and white—especially in the area of business ethics. Call a lawyer before blowing the whistle. And if you insist on blowing that whistle, know that your career is going to have a steep climb for a while afterward.

Sometimes the wrong fit is one in which you're stuck in a nowhere company, maybe one with an outdated product or obsolete technology. If the company is perceived as stodgy and stuck in the old ways, you could be perceived that way as well. One student of mine came to visit me for an informational interview. One look at her résumé told me she was going to face that problem. She was young, in her early thirties, bright, attractive, and highly educated. The only problem was that she had invested thirteen years of her young professional life in a company that was perceived for fifty miles in every direction as a has-been. Result: She couldn't even get an interview anywhere. "What should I do?" she asked, knowing that I might not be able to help her find a job, but that perhaps I could give her some insight.

As it turned out, I was able to help her. One of my clients, Oracle, happened to need a contract HR manager for a short assignment. At the time Oracle was growing rapidly and had a ratio of seven hundred employees to one HR person, which was unheard of. HR was tremendously overworked and they needed help. So I called her with the news: "There's this contract job I just heard about," I said. "It's a much longer commute than what you're used to. The employee to HR ratio is terrible. People are overworked and worn out. It doesn't pay well. There's no guarantee that it will lead to anything long term."

"So what are the other reasons you think I should take this job?" she said. At least she hadn't lost her sense of humor!

My answer: "It gets something on your résumé that's current. Oracle offers experience in an environment with sexier, emerging technology. If they offer you a regular, full-time position, take it. Stay there twenty-four months. Then you can put a great company name on your résumé and demonstrate that you can apply your profession in a new, hot company. And then you can go anywhere in your career."

And so she did.

2. BAD TIMING

When I was in the HR department of Western Digital Corp., we acquired a number of other companies. And with the stroke of a pen, entire HR departments were eliminated, and my department would absorb all their work. Once, in particular, I called my outgoing counterpart and told her, "I want to make this work for you." I committed to support her through her transition and she committed to transition her function over to me smoothly. And she went on to become the senior vice president of a major global, multi-billion-dollar company.

She had managed to take an awful situation and turn it into a huge success story. There was no shame in her predicament. She was simply at the losing end of an acquisition situation. Her main ally, the CEO of the acquired company, was also departing, and she had to watch her entire group be dismantled, throwing many people out of work.

While other people in her position may have held out for a top HR spot in a company of similar size, she decided to take a different approach. She took on the role of director in a bigger, more established company. And from that position of strength she was able to move ahead, to assume the top HR executive position less than ten years later. From a title standpoint, it may have appeared to be a setback. From a career standpoint, it put her exactly where she wanted to be.

Bad timing can be a horrible way to misstep. There's no guarantee that a hiring company will tell you that the position they desperately need you to fill today will be abolished when that particular organization is acquired and merged. Some employers may be able to earmark another spot for you to move into once the merger is completed. But can you count on it? Things have a way of changing as mergers evolve. Sometimes they have great intentions, but things just don't turn out as anticipated.

Sometimes your new company is acquired by the company you just left! It happens again and again. In this age of frequent consolidations, your old employer just may emerge to become your new employer once again. Surprise!

And then, of course, there are world events and the ups and downs of the economy. A friend of mine took a great job in a promising new company. His start date: September 10, 2001. This particular company was in an industry sector that was especially badly hit by the tragedy of the following day. It couldn't survive. It disappeared and so did his job.

When these events of bad timing spoil your best-laid plans, you can only shrug your shoulders and be as philosophical as possible about it. It's not about you. No one did this to you personally. And it's not about any bad decision you might have made or some reckless leap you committed before checking the landing pad. These things happen.

The more you take it personally, or use this as one more example to prove that you're just plain unlucky, the more it could become a self-fulfilling prophecy. An episode of bad timing may slow you down ever so slightly. But don't let it trip you up.

3. POOR JUDGMENT

Of course, some poor timing is predictable. (A dying industry, for example, is not a good place to launch your career.)

Other examples of bad judgment may include leaving a perfectly good company to go after a loftier title in a far lesser employer—either in industry stature or stability. You rarely want to choose to take a top position in a C company instead of a lesser job in an A company (we'll get to the discussion about A companies in the next chapter).

Poor judgment could also include ignoring the warning signs of the HR predecessors who have come and gone before you. One company I know has had seven vice presidents of HR in eight years. One lasted only three months. I have to wonder what Vice Presidents 5, 6, and 7 were thinking that made them hope it would be different with them. What is it that they thought they could change that their predecessors couldn't? The sad thing is that by the time you read this the company will probably have already cycled through Vice Presidents 8 through 10.

Joining a company with a bad reputation for its HR department or the way it treats people is also an example of bad judgment. If it has a poor reputation for the HR work it does, you will be tarnished with the label of "low standards." Hiring managers would be very reasonable to ask themselves, "Why would I want to hire anyone from there?"

If you're in that kind of company and can't afford to have another "job hop" on your résumé, stay there as long as you need to to demonstrate stability and progressive career growth. And then get out. Maximize whatever experience this particular company has to offer you, for instance, implementation of a brand-new HR information technology (HRIT) system. That way your time there won't be completely wasted.

In the time you are there, work toward neutralizing their reputation by doing incredible work. And then broadcast it. Network, go to meetings, speak at association gatherings, write articles for publication. Do whatever you can to attach a positive, progressive association to your name. If you stay insular, all they're going to see is the company's reputation. Build your own reputation independent of the company's image. You *can* build a great reputation by doing great things in a not-very-good company.

4. THE WRONG FRIENDS

While you were growing up, some adult probably told you that you're known by the company you keep. You are evaluated as having the same caliber of excellence as the people you socialize with. It stays just as true no matter how old you are. You want to choose your business friends carefully. Just as you want to dress for success, you also want to associate for success.

If you find yourself in social and business circles that sustain themselves by complaining, rehashing the latest outrages at work, and gossiping, extricate yourself from that environment as quickly as you can. As an HR professional, you must always be above reproach and suspicion. And when people overhear a group that you happen to be a part of speaking in low-quality ways about company business, they're going to assume you are actually taking part in the discussion. It's time for you to find new circles to move around in.

Seek out positive, upbeat, high-quality employees and colleagues. Be about the solutions, not the problems. Be sincerely interested in who they are as people, not just the reflected glory that would benefit you. And bring something of genuine value to "the party." What value do you bring to the group? Insight? Information? Creative solutions? Maybe even just a sincere hope for a real friendship. It doesn't have to be much, but it does have to be genuine.

If you tend to be shy and introverted, don't let that slow you down. I have found that HR professionals are more introverted than they'd like to admit. As a result, their networks are very insular, feeding on one another rather than bringing fresh influences and contributions into the group. If you find that you're having lunch or drinks with the same group every week, you can be pretty sure that you're not building the networks of people who can help support your long-term career goals over the decades.

I don't mean that you should only associate with people who are helpful to you in your career. Just try to associate with a broader base of people so that career opportunities can come to you. It will happen.

5. THE WRONG COMPANY

A demoralizing business circle is bad enough. A morally or legally loose one is altogether hazardous. Turning a blind eye to questionable practices can wreck an HR career. It's shocking how many HR leaders have stories to tell about the moment when they had to take a stand against their corporate leadership, at great risk of their careers. But when they realize that the alternative puts their personal freedom at significant risk, the choice is clear. It might not be any easier, but it's unmistakable.

Reflecting back on one of those moments at a previous employer, Marianne Jackson, vice president, HR, of Palm, had this to say: "I was in a difficult situation at one time, but felt I had to take a stand. It was one of those situations that, today, would have raised some serious red flags. I stood my ground and it cost me. But I can sleep at night, and I did recover. Being courageous is really hard, and you could pay a price for it. But I've also known people who didn't show courage and paid a career price. Show courage."

6. POLITICAL MISTAKES

Every company has politics. And HR is probably one of the functions that is most vulnerable to political struggles. You often have to work across functions and help differing interests find common ground. It's not uncommon for HR professionals and their departments to get reputations for being political—and that's not a good thing. Other departments and functions don't trust them. They don't confide in HR. And as a result they don't use HR's services very effectively.

The HR day is filled with all sorts of situations and problems, and many of them can actually bring with them very unpleasant circumstances for the employees. It's okay to try to put a positive spin on a bad situation, but HR must always be clear, honest, and up front, even in the most difficult of situations. There is a difference between presenting things in a positive way and being dishonest.

This is especially important when HR finds itself again and again having to support one side of an issue over another. In HR, you can't be seen taking the middle of the road when the going gets tough. There is an old saying that goes like this: "Man who walks down middle of road gets hit by traffic going in both directions." You're going to have to take a stand. And for every stand you take, there is a side that will remember that you didn't support their argument.

Those are the people who will never forget that (A) you did your best, or (B) you burned them. What they remember is up to you. It's far better to take these people aside and privately say to them, "Look, I have given this situation a tremendous amount of thought. I must take a stand on this situation, and I hope you won't take this personally. It's not about you or our relationship. This is what I think is best for the business. I want you to know ahead of time where I stand on this."

Maybe you won't be best friends for life, but you won't be enemies either.

If you can, be the person to bring the opposite sides of a disagreement to common ground. Be solution-oriented without compromising your values or theirs. Regardless of the argument, always try to rise above the fray.

Don't harbor grudges. This is a business; it's a job. It's not all that important in the overall scheme of life. The world isn't going to end because of a single situation. But your career could get stalled if years from now someone on the hiring committee remembers that time when you . . . .

If you're already embroiled in a political mess, you may or may not be able to recover in your own company. But give yourself the chance to make things right before moving on. Go back to the wounded party, acknowledge the situation, and say something like, "Look, this didn't work out the way I was hoping it would. Do you think we can both get past it?"

Do what you can do to build the bridges. Time can take care of that sometimes. It's harder to regain trust once you've lost it. Don't let it happen the second time. You can recover once, but not twice.

7. INAPPROPRIATE AGE

You can't help your age, so it's hardly fair to call it a misstep. But letting your age get in the way of achieving your ambitions *might* be a misstep. Being perceived as either too young or too old can be equally difficult. A person who is too young can be perceived as not having had enough life experience. And truly, some things can only be learned through life experience. There's only so much you can read in books and hear from other people. Some things you really have to experience yourself to have that seasoning and maturity to take certain levels of leadership roles inside a company.

There's not much you can do about being too young. Think about work experiences that you've had and be ready to talk about contributions you've made and how you've prepared yourself. Volunteer for as many leadership opportunities as you can squeeze into your life. Each one will add much value to you as a candidate for a leadership-bound position.

Another approach you can take is to be sure you appear as you wish to be perceived—as a professional with some years of experience behind you. When I was younger in my career, when I and my peers got a few gray hairs, we left them in. We considered them a huge plus at that stage of our career. And the old rule of thumb survives today: Always dress to the position to which you aspire.

I don't think most companies care about age when it comes to maturing employees. They care about energy, creativity, innovativeness. Most of the time, it's not an age problem; it's a mindset problem. But if you are worried that you might be too old, there are a number of things you can do. Do what you can to look fresh, energetic, contemporary, and attentive. Perhaps you might go to an image consultant to get some advice. It's easy to lose sight of what we really look like after years of the same old habits in our grooming. For women, it's easier because we can do things with make-up and clothes. For men, it's a little more difficult. But it's mostly about being in the best physical condition possible, being well-dressed in up-to-date styles (if your suit is fifteen years old, you know what to do with it, right?), and having an energetic, upbeat personality. Some people with significant years of experience come across mature, energetic, bright, creative, and knowledgeable. Others come across as old. Which do you want to come across as? And then prepare your image for that. You can't change your age, but you can change your image.

Is it harder for someone over fifty to find great career opportunities? Sure, it's harder. But why? Many people make their age a barrier by allowing their age to be more of a factor than it needs to be.

8. DERAILING PRIORITIES

Again, this may not be a misstep. You have other priorities in life, and some of them may take you out of the working world for a little while. Just know that some absence from the "happening" scene may push you back a few years. And then you might have to exert a little more energy getting back into it than you originally anticipated. Whatever the reason you decide to back-burner your career for the sake of other priorities, it will have some ramifications.

Removing yourself from the corporate world for consulting isn't necessarily going to work against you. Stepping off the track to have children may not hurt you, as long as it is only for a year or two. But as we've already discussed, some people who stepped out of the workforce during the recent boom took a very long time to get back in the game when the boom ended. Timing can be important.

Do whatever it takes to get back in the swing of things. Once you're in, do what you can to surge forward as quickly as possible to regain some of your lost ground.

Say that you are back from Costa Rica now and discover that it's probably going to take you about another year to find your next job (and that you have the financial resources to stick it out). Filling that time in meaningful ways will protect you from the misstep of having nothing to say about your current self when interview season comes around again.

One HR leader I know donated her expertise to nonprofits that were important to her. She got involved on the board of the private school her children went to. She upgraded her skills with important and relevant nonprofit work. Another person I know began work on her Ph.D. On her résumé, it shows that she continued a great track record of professional growth. In the interviews, all she had to say about her additional education was, "This is something I always wanted to do. I had an opportunity to work on my education. And I could afford it. So that's what I did."

A gap in your job history is okay if it's well-timed, planned, and executed. Be able to demonstrate the value of the gap. Stay connected. Contact peers. Do interviews. Conduct a survey that would give you an excuse to call your colleagues. Volunteer to do interviewing workshops at your local community center. This extracurricular activity—especially a self-designed project that is both high-level and appeals to your passion—could take you far in positioning yourself as a substantial candidate who is a solid, forward-thinking citizen who leads growth in the community.

9. YOU DIDN'T SEE THE HANDWRITING ON THE WALL

There's something bad going on in your company, and for some reason you're just plain not seeing it. It could be related to a financial situation, where you stand with the executive team yourself, or HR's reputation. Maybe a new CEO coming in wants to install her own chief HR leader, and you're not it. Maybe there's an SEC investigation that could tarnish the company's name and yours too.

If there is handwriting on the wall, you'd better spot it quickly. And then you'd better take the proactive approach to dealing with it, before it deals with you. Again, it's important to have a plan of action. What will be the new circumstances under which you're going to move your career forward? Do you want to go? Do you want to stay? Continue to do a good job and work the dynamics so that when you decide to exit, you can do it with grace. Get yourself out there, looking for the next opportunity.

Sometimes there are situations where the handwriting is on the wall and you just can't talk about it. Sensitive downsizing plans, for example. Or SEC investigations, for another. You can still refer to them in oblique terms, assuming you have a good relationship with a trusted recruiter. That recruiter should appreciate that the topic is sensitive and should be able to give you the necessary advice you need to answer questions as fully as possible without creating a damaging indiscretion. You can still be getting your name out there as someone who is interested in hearing about new opportunities without divulging sensitive information. If recruiters or search committees come too close to sensitive areas in their questioning, simply say to them, "There's a situation that I can't talk about at the moment. I'd be crossing an ethical line here. When I am able to tell you more, I will. But I can't cross that ethical line right now."

That response alone will answer a very important question that search committees will have about you: Are you trustworthy and discreet?

No one is immune from missing the handwriting on the wall. I was doing some work for an HR vice president one time when we were about to present an offer to a new compensation director. All we had left to do was verbally close on the details. But he called me that afternoon, saying, "I have to cancel tomorrow's breakfast. We're not going through with the offer." I was naturally very surprised and, of course, disappointed.

"I have to tell you something," he continued, then he told me he had received an invoice for a search from another company and he didn't know what it was. So he called the company to find out what the invoice was for, thinking it was some sort of error. Answer: It was for *his* job. The CEO had started a search to replace him. And he obviously didn't know he was being replaced.

Over the previous months, this CEO had replaced everyone on the executive team, except for him. He was the only one left standing. He thought he had done a great job forging relationships with the new team and that he had somehow escaped the fate of the other members of his original team. And now, with this invoice clutched in his hand, he had only one conclusion: "I obviously cannot stay here." He went to the CEO, taking the invoice with him. "I don't understand," he said. "I thought things were working great."

The CEO squirmed. "We were just testing the waters," he said. And the HR vice president correctly refused to buy that. You don't spend $50,000 to $100,000 on a search without intending to hire someone. You don't window shop with that kind of money.

For the HR vice president, it became an issue of trust more than one of job security. He handled it very professionally, telling his CEO that the time had obviously come for him to leave, and that it was now a question of designing a departure that was dignified. He handled it very professionally, negotiated a severance package, and left.

His misstep was that he didn't assess his relationship with the CEO and the team very well from the beginning. He allowed himself to believe that somehow he would be the exception. Was it ego? Or was it wishful thinking? It doesn't really matter. The reality worked out the same. He missed the handwriting on the wall, costing himself a gap of more than a year.

10. YOUR REPUTATION'S RUINED

People in HR are nowhere if their reputation isn't impeccable. What you do about a ding or a smudge depends on why it's damaged. If it's attached to a company that has found itself in trouble—either in legal court or the court of public opinion—you can try to separate your reputation from the company's. Don't stay too long in a company that doesn't have a great reputation, unless you can change it. If you can change it, terrific! You've really enhanced your value in the market. Recruiters and search committees could say, "If you could have a positive impact there, just think what you can do in a great company." If you can change it, change it. If you can't, do the best you can do. Stay one to two years, and use that experience to go to a better employer.

While you're waiting out those years, choose extracurricular activities to neutralize whatever stigma is attached to you as a result of your association with that company.

The last thing you want to do is mess up your own personal reputation. Improving your personal reputation is harder. If your own name is tarnished because of ethics, poor communication, or poor relationship building, you really need to do a self-evaluation. You can change it; it just takes time. Personal reputations change very slowly.

First, recognize the situation and plan ways to deal with it. Find a personal evangelist. Mend fences. Change market sectors. Create a series of projects, each one more successful than the last. Let that kind of word-of-mouth replace the bad stories attached to your name.

Be forewarned though. If your reputation is that you're dishonest, that's going to be a lot harder to overcome. If a CFO steals money, no one is going to hire him as a CFO again. You may be able to find a job on your own, but if your résumé crosses my recruiter's desk and I've heard of your indiscretion, I probably would not present you to any client companies. Why should I? I can find better candidates who don't have a tarnished track record. That may sound terribly harsh, but a recruiter's job is not to rehabilitate HR professionals who need a leg up again after doing their penance. Our job is to serve our client companies by gathering the best possible selection of candidates and then selecting only the best from that elite group to present to the client. You want to be in that group.

11. MOVE TOO FAST OR MOVE TOO SLOW

This means job hopping or staying too long. It's okay to move fast within a company. Inside a company it's recognition that you're really good and really smart and that you can quickly pick up what you don't know along the way. But you also run the risk of moving so fast that you neglect to acquire the necessary tools and basic experiences on the way up. You have to make sure you're squeezing all the knowledge and experience you can out of a role before moving on to the next one.

But going from company to company to company at hyper speed may be an indicator that you are good at selling yourself but not delivering. Maybe you are bailing before they figure you out. Or maybe they figured you out and you're on your way out. You're just staying one step ahead of disaster.

It's just as bad to move too slow, either within a company or externally. A compensation analyst I know stayed in the same job for seventeen years. That's too long if you want a career, as opposed to a job. And now, after so long, she found herself without the valuable knowledge and experience attached to progressive career growth that would make her marketable. She was caught flat-footed. She had one year's experience seventeen times. From a recruiter's perspective, it's impossible to market that kind of background.

It may be that you spend ten years perfectly happy in one specialty only to wake up one day to discover that your ambitions have completely changed. Now you want to work your way into a top HR slot before you retire. Uh oh. Time to get moving. Find a way to move into another functional area—a generalist role would be especially smart to balance out the long-term specialty focus you had been zeroing in on. In the meantime, get more in-depth knowledge in a few other specialty areas. You don't necessarily have to have working experience in all of them; you don't have that kind of time any more. But do take classes in those areas, and join networks of specialists from throughout your geographic region or industry. Build your database of contacts in the broad scope of all the HR functions. Then when you get to the vice president role, you can hire some of the people you met along the way.

Do it with a sense of purpose. Plan to gain knowledge. Work your plan, and try not to skip the essential steps along the way.

WRAP-UP

With any misstep, assume that the misstep is visible. When you're out there interviewing, be prepared to deal with it and talk about it as a situation you have learned from. You don't necessarily have to bring it up as a misstep, but be prepared to talk about what you would have done differently and what you would do to avoid that situation in the future.

Keep in mind that careers are long, and your chances of fumbling now and then are, unfortunately, fairly high. That's when it helps to be philosophical, knowing that you're only human in a deeply human-oriented profession. With patience, flexibility, willingness to compromise your immediate expectations for the sake of your long-term goals, and the ability to tell your story from the heart and from a healthy perspective, there is just about nothing that you can't overcome.

SUMMARY

- There are very few missteps that you can't recover from—those that have ethical, honesty, or trust implications.
- When explaining what happened to you in the past, the truth is always the best option. Just be careful to be diplomatic and tactful about the people involved in your past.
- Be philosophical. You're a human being in a deeply human profession. Forgive yourself with the understanding that well-intentioned errors tell the story of someone growing and learning.

INTERVIEW

Ann Rhoades

President, PeopleInk; one of the five founding leaders and current board member, JetBlue; Former Vice President/People of Southwest Airlines; and Executive Vice President/People of Doubletree Hotels

WHILE CONCLUDING a high-pressure stint as executive vice president of people for Doubletree Hotels, Ann Rhoades decided it was finally time to launch her Phoenix-based consulting firm, PeopleInk. She had already committed to the office space, and two associates were already there hard at work. But a series of persistent phone calls from a former Southwest Airlines co-worker sent her in a new and totally unexpected direction: the planning and launch of a brand new airline, JetBlue.

In 2004, JetBlue is an established player in a field in which successful start-ups are rare under the best of circumstances, but the post–September 11, 2001, economy was especially brutal to airlines. Although she has passed the full-time responsibilities to her personally recruited successor, she remains active on JetBlue's board. She is also a board member of another post–New Economy success story: PF Chang's China Bistro, an up-market Asian restaurant brand, as well as the privately held Western Warehouse, a western apparel chain store throughout the Southwest.

In this interview she talks about the necessity of being able to take risks, even if it means putting your job on the line.

What is the best piece of advice you ever received?

Always be a risk taker. I once reported to a CEO who was a very poor example of leadership. He was not particularly good at the financial side, and he certainly wasn't good with the people side. Before long, it became clear at the corporate level that the bank just wasn't getting the results we should have, so they sent in a senior player I didn't know at all. He arranged private meetings with the entire staff, and my appointment just happened to be over dinner one night. He asked my opinion about whether we should retain the CEO and I said, "Absolutely not." I decided that rather than work for someone who wasn't an example of what I wanted to aspire to, I was going to tell this guy the truth—and accept the consequences.

Then I went home and told my husband I probably didn't have a job anymore.

But to my amazement, the very next day, the CEO was let go. I was the only one on the senior team who told the corporate representative the truth. Later on he said to me, "Thank you. Everyone else was trying to cover it up because they were worried about their jobs." Other than myself, there wasn't a living soul who told him the truth.

This is my big concern about people in HR. I think we have become a group of people who are not known for taking risks. Over the years CEOs have come to expect HR professionals to be people who don't speak up. The new breed say they do, but I've been around them and, believe me, a lot of them don't—even in the large corporations.

You have to be a risk taker, but you have to get inside the organization and build the necessary trust and respect first. Then little by little you have to start forwarding your opinions. If they aren't accepted, I'd no more stay there than the man in the moon. A risk taker has to be respected.

What was the moment your career changed forever?

My career changed when I went from the trust department of the bank to the people side of the organization. I finally had a direction that I loved. Prior to that I had been working on the financial side of the trust department as an analyst, but I found I had more fun with the customers. Moving over there brought out in me what my greatest talent is: Working with people.

I was immediately regarded as someone who was not a "typical" HR person.

I consider HR to be very closely related to marketing. You're always selling something: Your ability to help operations, your company's opportunity to attract A Players. Getting A Players is the most important thing we can do for any company. Most A Players want to play with A Players. And if you play with them you can successfully achieve things that would make other people say, "No way!"

When we started JetBlue, we knew that our A Players were going to ensure its success—even after something so devastating as September 11. The people made it. The idea didn't make it. The concept didn't make it. The venture capitalists didn't make it. The people made it, the ones who every day interacted with those customers, whether it's the first interaction on the phone, whether it's when they got to the airport, or they get off the aircraft, it's every single interaction.

What is the best piece of advice you have to offer up-and-comers in the HR profession?

Early on, take some calculated risks. Tell people what you really believe. Don't ever couch something for the person you report to. Never be afraid to risk your job. Never. You're risking a great deal more than that when you don't tell people what you believe and you don't give them your opinion.

What do they need now that you didn't need when you started in HR?

I wasn't expected to be a financial expert. You'd better know a lot about it today. Some might say you need a grounding in law. Don't worry about that. You'll learn everything you need to know about law on the job. You have to know law, but you learn it very quickly. I've learned a lot just by sitting with my lawyers. But you should be equipped with knowledge about the finance side coming into the profession.

What's the best thing that new entrants into the profession should do for themselves?

Get operational experience in whatever arena you're in. It will give you a whole different point of view that will be useful, even if you change industry sectors. And it will give you credibility.

What's the worst thing?

Think like an HR person (as opposed to a businessperson).

What do you look for when hiring HR professionals?

I look for a great answer when I ask the question: "Give me an example of the time you broke a rule for an employee." If the person can't think of five examples, I don't hire him or her. I want the example, and I want to know what the result was. And then I want to know about the next time he or she broke another rule.

Would you say there is more gray area in HR than in any other part of the company? More judgment calls? More opportunities for mistakes?

You're asked to make judgment calls all the time. And you're the person they would love to blame the first time something goes wrong. You need to be more flexible than anyone else in the company and have the ability to move with the organization fast. The ones who are successful are pretty fast moving, even at a time when everyone else isn't. A lot of people aren't flexible in HR because they were taught not to be early on in their careers. It drives me crazy.

What risk have you taken recently that paid off?

I had just started my consulting company in Phoenix, and immediately went to New York for three years to start JetBlue. I thought it was a great opportunity. I had done a lot of things, but I had not started up a large organization the way I thought it should be from a people values and customer service side. There were only ten people when I got there. Now there are 6,000.

And it paid off! I learned a valuable lesson: You can create a great people organization with the right players anywhere. These days, it's not too difficult to exceed expectations. But once you exceed them, to keep doing it is very difficult. But it will happen with the right players.

Would you say there is no shame in calling yourself a people person as long as you can back it up with business acumen?

There's shame in terms of other people thinking it's too warm and fuzzy and doesn't mean a thing. I don't think there's any shame when you're able to execute on it and show that in a customer service environment you better have a lot of *people* people.

If someone says he or she's a *people* person, then he'd better *be* one. And still better have the competencies for the job. A *people* person to me isn't just someone who can glad-hand you and say hello and feel comfortable with you. He or she has to do whatever it takes to help make that business successful.

In addition, I don't believe you can have people who work with you who aren't your friends.

INTERVIEW

David Russo

President, Eno River Associates; Former Vice President, Human Resources (retired), SAS Institute

DAVID RUSSO WOULDN'T know it at the time, of course, but early in his career he put himself directly on the path of extraordinary success when he turned down the promise of job security for the sake of loyalty to a former employer. Because of that decision, he would eventually become the first head of HR for SAS Institute, the world's largest privately held software company. And SAS, in turn, would become celebrated for its people practices during David's tenure there, even achieving the rare honor of actually being featured positively by 60 Minutes. *Under his direction SAS Institute was named in* Fortune *magazine's Top Ten Best Companies to Work For for four consecutive years, and it placed ten times on* Working Mother *magazine's list of 100 Best Companies for Working Mothers.*

Today he is the founder and head of Eno River Associates, a Durham, North Carolina, employee engagement consulting firm, helping other companies implement workforce strategies to attract and retain competitive talent in their markets.

In this interview David talks about the importance of making decisions independently of what the been-there-done-that experts will advise and about building your career based on specific expertise and then growing from that point.

What is the best advice you have ever received?

It's a combination of business and personal advice. Harry Dawley, a former boss, told me, "Make it your business to live 10 percent below your income." Most of the people around you are living

10 percent or more *above* their income. As a result, their lives are stressful for a variety of reasons, primarily because they will always be straining to merit that lifestyle. It's more than just a mathematical issue. It's also a psychological issue. When you live 10 percent below your income, you will have accumulated a cushion over the years that makes decisions about purchasing, lifestyle, career, family, even decisions about ethics, far easier. If something doesn't smell right, you're not compelled to stay associated with it by the fact that someone has you by the financial throat.

Did it make me rich? No. But it's made me much more secure than I might have been.

What was the moment when your career changed forever?

It was the summer of 1981, and I heard that SAS Institute was growing rapidly beyond its base of a few people and had fifty employees. I wrote to Jim Goodnight, owner and president, and reminded him that we had met through my wife, Marsha. I wrote, "You're getting to the size where you may need HR help. I'm here if you need me." The letter prompted a meeting, and I asked him what his expectations were. And he said, "I expect you to help me build the kind of company where I would like to be an employee."

The vision of being a great place to work was his. The vision of *working* to make an organization a great place to work was mine. So we were in synch.

What is the one thing you wish you had done differently?

I wish I had been less influenced by people who had *been there and done that* in my early years. So many of these HR people were just going through the motions. Their operating philosophy seemed to be: "We do it this way today because we did it that way yesterday." Because I was new I was very heavily influenced not to rock the boat, or "shake the box," as I call it. I wish I had started shaking that box a lot earlier and not waited until I was the primary influencer of HR strategy and tactics to do that. I think I would have been a lot happier in my early days.

Do we typically wait too long until we have that seniority before we give ourselves permission to shake the proverbial box? Are we waiting for some kind of graduation ceremony?

Most people don't ever shake the box because they never get to the point where they feel they have the necessary authority. The sad thing is that some people get so comfortable with that "been there/done that" working environment that they never break away from it. And then they go on to become impediments to the next generation of junior people.

What is the best piece of advice you have to offer those on the way up?

Be an active listener. Learn from everyone. It may be something you're going to use, or it may be something you promise yourself you're *never* going to use. It all is valuable. Learn from the best. Learn from the worst. Learn from the average. Everyone has something to offer.

And then after you've learned from everyone, be yourself. Don't be anyone else. Be as genuine as you can be. If you are, you'll always be able to sleep at night. You'll always be able to get out of bed in the morning with a spring in your step, and you'll always be able to look people in the eye and be authentic. You won't have to remember what you said to someone or how you behaved in a previous situation.

What do up-and-coming professionals need now that you didn't need when you started in your HR career?

Up-and-coming HR professionals need three things:

First, they need platform skills. HR people should be good at thinking on their feet and making persuasive presentations on a moment-by-moment basis. It wasn't a requirement when I was coming up through the ranks. We just had to keep our heads down and focus on the forms. The only people who needed good platform skills then were labor negotiators.

Second, they should know, understand, and be able to apply statistical theories and principles. The ability to present and analyze data is what will be the power base of HR in the future. This is the way they will be required to prove their business cases. HR has been a storehouse of data for many years. But most HR professionals have never been able to make compelling business cases or present succinct reports based on the data they've stored because they don't have the skills or the interest in doing the statistical analysis necessary to build their cases. It's always been "Trust me, I just know it's so," based on anecdotal information. That's not very compelling in this day and age when everyone else at the table is sitting there with reams and reams of statistical analysis.

And third, they really need to understand business, the principles of how businesses are run, how they make money, and how human capital adds value. We've been saying it for years. So many HR people I've known don't have a grip on their company, how they're run, or even how their products work or provide service or value. They're just *people* people, and there's a lack of alignment between what they do and what the company is all about. There's also a lack of alignment between what they do and business in general.

What is the best thing new entrants can do for themselves?

They should find an area of HR where they can establish some kind of expertise and go after it. In your early years, you get opportunities by having a recognized skill within the silos of HR. That way you become the valuable, visible expert that the organization leans on. That's a career builder.

But it's also important not to become pigeon-holed. And the way you control that is by showing interest and expertise across the general scope of HR and the business.

So become valuable for what you can contribute in a special area, but at the same time, be better than just conversant in all the general areas. And then people will never see you as a specialist. They'll see you as a generalist with a special skill, or two, or three.

What is the worst thing that they can do?

Put themselves between the employees and the management. For too many people in too many organizations, HR is either management's cudgel or the employees' defender. As a result, nobody trusts HR in those companies. They're basically a double agent. Both sides have to understand that HR is a profession, and its role is to serve the organization. Management and employees both are the organization, and so whatever HR does should be what's best for the organization.

If you were to hire a new HR professional today, what characteristics and qualities would you be looking for?

Unbridled enthusiasm. I would be looking for someone who is looking for a job and not the position. It's not a *position,* it's plain hard work to be in human resources. People are going to disappoint you. They're going to back-stab you. They're going to uplift you. They're going to amaze you. And how are you going to deal with all those emotions if you really just want the position because you "love dealing with people?" Come to HR with enthusiasm, wanting to do the work, and with the understanding that companies are nothing more than lots and lots of people with a single purpose. And your job is to help them deliver that purpose.

What was the biggest risk you took in your career that paid off?

In 1979, Liggett Group, the consumer products company I was working for at the time, chose to move its corporate headquarters from Durham, North Carolina, to Montvale, New Jersey. I was among the group of professionals invited to go. I was offered a salary nearly twice what I was making here, a bonus, and relocation help. They offered me the opportunity to live and work in the corporate center of the world. But I had fallen in love with the South, its people, and the atmosphere here. So I turned them down without having another job to go to. It wasn't long before I accepted a new job in Florida that was to begin on August 1. But while I was still at Liggett, my boss came to me and said, "The transition period ends August 20, and I'd really appreciate it if you stayed until then." So I called my new company and said, "I'm so thankful that you gave me this opportunity, and I really want this job. But could I have a three-week respite? My company is shutting down here and my boss, to whom I owe some loyalty, has asked me to stay to help."

The guy who hired me said, "Nope. We made a deal. Come on August 1 or don't come at all."

And I called him back the next day and said, "I'm not coming."

So without a job to fall back on, I stayed with my boss until August 20 to turn out the lights. But if I hadn't done what felt to be morally and loyally the right thing to do, I would never have had the opportunity with SAS.

6

CONTROL WHAT YOU CAN; LET THE REST GO

While most of the aspects and elements of your career are entirely within your control to improve on or change altogether, there are some areas that are completely beyond your ability to alter. This chapter outlines those areas, providing you with suggestions on how you can at least mitigate their negative effects.

ONE GOVERNING PRINCIPLE throughout this book is that you have more control over your career than you think you do. This isn't to cast doubt on your knowledge of your market or your understanding of how your skills and experiences match with the expectations of recruiters and employers today. The simple reality is that in my decades in HR and then as a recruiter and HR consultant, I have not met many people who are completely confident that they are in the driver's seat when it comes to knowing that their next best job is out there waiting for them. As I've said earlier in the book, even in down markets there will be plenty of excellent jobs out there waiting to be filled by quality candidates.

My hope is, of course, that by this point in the book you have a stronger understanding about the overall HR landscape and confidence in driving your career decisions and choices. But even with all this added sense of command over your career, both short term and long term, there are still some elements that are truly beyond your capacity to control. And the only thing you can control about these elements is your attitude about them, how much you might be willing to adjust yourself around them, and how quickly you can get really philosophical and let go of those details that simply resist your efforts.

THE ALLURE OF THE "A PLAYER"

One element you can't control is that irresistible power of the elusive A Player. Every company that retains me to do their search always takes a moment in the conversation to specify, "Bring us only A Players. We only hire A Players." This is always just a little strange to me. I understand that they want only the best, who can do the work brilliantly. But the fact that they feel they must actually *specify* the request must come from the same place where we keep the compulsion to push the elevator button even though it's already lit and been pushed by the fifteen people waiting for the elevator too. After all, who knowingly would hire a B Player?

In other words: You don't ask; you don't get.

In point of fact, there is no universal standard for an A Player. And, from a search committee's perspective, chasing after the satisfaction that you've hired one is like chasing after a fine scarf in a brisk wind. It will always seem tantalizingly just out of reach.

And from a candidate's point of view, you can design your career as planfully as an engineer, and still find yourself just askew of expectations from the search committee that holds your dream job in its hands. With every career choice that you make with every passing day, you are creating the story of your life's work. And even though each decision is the best one available to you at each moment with the knowledge and foresight that you have at the time, one choice, one instant when you looked out the window instead of down at the work on your desk, could land you squarely in the B Player category in the estimation of the search committee. That's not something you can control. And you'll make yourself nuts if you try.

Let's look at how the definition of "A Player" often breaks down in the minds of search committee members:

EDUCATION. Sometimes committee members care most about the candidate's level of education. That is within your control. But sometimes it's the specific schools the candidates have attended. Unless you were lucky enough to know you wanted to be in business, and specifically in HR, from the time you were very young, chances are excellent that you didn't aggressively seek out the best schools for HR or business programs: Cornell, Stanford, Harvard, University of Michigan, and others. In fact, if you're middle-aged as you read this book, you'll remember that most schools didn't even have a formal HR program when you went to school. If you're an older candidate with, say, a B.A. in art history, and you wandered into HR and fell in love with the profession, you're no less qualified, no less passionate about your work simply because you didn't receive your degree in industrial relations from Cornell.

You can mitigate that knick in your résumé if you want to. It's never too late to get an MBA, if you have the time, ambition, and focus to pursue one. I've had people say to me, "I'm already in my thirties; what's the point?" My response is to remind them that they'll probably be in their careers until at least sixty-five. That's thirty years of opportunity to make use of that degree!

If getting that degree is important to you, pick the best school that you can. Many excellent schools offer MBA programs as night courses for working adults. Find the best-rated program that's accessible to you and pursue that credential.

The question of distance learning programs has come up repeatedly over the years. It's too soon to evaluate their true effectiveness in giving candidates that extra competitive edge with search committees. But because the HR profession has such a strong human component to it, I would say that, whatever distance learning classes you pursue, make sure they're balanced with classes and other opportunities in which you have face-to-face interaction, in order to grow your interpersonal skills and experiences. In addition, make sure that these courses are affiliated with top-rated schools.

THE CALIBER OF COMPANIES THE CANDIDATES COME FROM. Sometimes search committee members define A Players according to the stature of the companies that are already on their résumé—top companies in their industry or community or some other defined segment. This is sometimes difficult for candidates to anticipate and control in advance. Associating with winners makes you a winner. But it's not always easy to predict who the winners are going to be.

True, there are some unquestionably stellar players in every industry category. If you want to be competitive in the corporate level of retail, time spent in the corporate office at Gap, Nordstrom, Nieman-Marcus, Borders, or Barnes and Noble will make your résumé unquestionably desirable to other big-name stores. But these companies are so big that you may have exposure to one narrow HR specialty inside that corporation, and the search committee of the moment is looking for candidates who have a broader-based exposure to all the functions within HR because this particular company likes to keep its HR department small and strategic, outsourcing as much of the tactical work as possible.

That's their definition of an A Player, and that's not something you can control. You may have to let that go.

Or you can know in advance that your ambition is to grow start-ups in retail and so you front-load the first ten to fifteen years of your career with as broad a variety of HR opportunities in the retail space as you can, in hopes that one day a search committee will come along and ask for someone just like you. And that that particular recruiter has your résumé in her files. It's been known to happen, but that skirts awfully close to the right-time-right-place magical formula that's really completely out of your control.

Chasing after what other people perceive to be A Player companies could be a lifelong frustration for you, if you decide to build your résumé in this manner. It's far better for you to decide how A Player companies are defined according to *your* criteria and stand by that—knowing full well, of course, that you can change your mind as your lengthy career life spools itself out. True, you can't control the search committees' expectations of A Players from A Player companies, but you can control your experience in the companies that represent the A category to *you*. In general, I recommend that you seek out the Number One or Number Two company in an industry that interests *you*, that *you* believe to have a bright future, and that has a great reputation for treating employees well. Ask around. Read what is published about them—the material that is *not* listed on their official websites.

If you decide to pursue your own version of A Player companies, it may mean that you will have to make other sacrifices. If you want to be in A Player high-tech companies, for instance, you may have to leave your beloved hometown (and friends and family) for the various "silicon" communities scattered throughout the country. If your identified A Player companies anticipate international assignments as part of their employee development programs, several assignments abroad may be a thrill for some but a hardship for you.

And if you're absolutely committed to filling your résumé with strictly A Player employers (again, according to *your* definition), I can almost guarantee that you will be forced to face anxiety squarely in the eye and be challenged to say, "No, thanks," to a B Player offer, even though there's no other prospect waiting in the pipeline. Holding out for your own A opportunities can be one of the most nerve-wracking aspects of your career story. But when you do hold in your own mind a clear definition of what A means to you, you may be able to help recruiters and search committee members redefine what A means to *them*. At the very least, as you progress through the many interviews in your career, you'll always be able to stick to your story, as I discussed in Chapter 2.

If you have the misfortune of being associated with a company that suffers a reputation hit along the way, rise above that particular battlefield and focus on your accomplishments and results. You can demonstrate your abilities to be successful despite the noise and detrimental news swirling around the company's name. With the guidance of skilled recruiters, search committees can rise to the challenge of being able to separate the player from the company in most cases. Just as a film critic can separate excellent acting from a bad script, thoughtful search committee members can separate quality HR professionalism from a bad company story—*provided* that you indeed represent quality HR professionalism.

THE CALIBER OF THE HR CANDIDATES THEMSELVES. A Player candidates are often defined as HR professionals who are able to identify important issues and bring to the table a selection of effective solutions. They are dedicated professionals confident enough in themselves to take risks; they are not afraid to try new things; and they are not afraid to fail. A Player candidates have a creative edge to them.

But it may not be you at this stage of your life. Maybe you reserve your risk budget for some other aspect of your life that holds more meaning for you and the promise of a more valuable personal return. Maybe in comparison to what you're facing in your private life, corporate adventure—even with its billions of dollars and thousands of jobs at stake—seems like child's play. And you just can't be distracted with your main reason for living at the moment, thank you very much. Again, the choice is yours, but the emphasis that the search committee places on the risk-taking executive may be beyond your availability to be dedicated and take risks in a corporate setting. You may have to let that one go. For now.

STELLAR REFERENCES. My business partner, Roshni Southard, has a wonderful expression for the ideal candidate: "100-percent referenceable." The idea is that we should strive to live our lives and perform our work in such a way that, no matter who the search committee bumps into on the street or calls about you, that person would sing your praises. While there's not a soul on this planet who doesn't have something negative that can be said about him or her, our ultimate goal is to leave a trail of co-workers, colleagues, customers, and bosses, all of whom would say good things about the work that we did.

This doesn't mean that you are universally beloved. But it does mean that every single person you've worked for or with would be able to point to his or her experience with you as an excellent time in his or her own working life. Such a reference could go like this: "I have to tell you that I didn't always agree with him; he's really tough. But I also learned more from him than anyone else I've worked with." That's a great reference.

In reality not everyone is going to say nice things about you. Every one of us has stories about people who have crossed our paths, people who just didn't see eye-to-eye with us on basic issues of life or work. They're not going to be your friends, and they're not going to be on your résumé as a contact for reference. But they could be called by search committee members for a "back-door reference." If you're around long enough in your profession, there will be an ever-growing circle of people who know people who know you—especially if you stay in a single industry or geographic area. Your search committee members assume that the three names on your résumé are going to give positive information about you. So they will seek out a more balanced appraisal by poking around the other circles of people who might know you to see what they have to say. That's beyond your control.

What is within your control is to make sure the balance of your circles of friends and associates is made up of positive, effective, upbeat, fair-minded individuals. You want to associate with those people as much as possible so that your pipeline of even back-door acquaintances is filled with people who typically say good things, period. You have a set number of hours in every day. The more time you spend with these people, the less time you have available for negative, critical people who won't be pleased no matter what you do. A Players spend their time with people who will enhance their lives, not detract from them. That's within your control.

OTHER ASPECTS WITHIN YOUR CONTROL

You can control your own expectations of yourself and your ambitions. Not everyone is cut out to be the senior vice president of HR for a major multinational conglomerate. This is a good thing, because actually there are only a few of those positions available anyway. Maybe you're best at being the senior vice president of HR for a small start-up. Or maybe you're the world's best staffing director for an international consulting firm. To be at the top of your game doesn't necessitate that you be at the top of a top company. It just means that you are the best at what you do.

Go where your passion calls you. You need to decide for yourself based on how excited you feel in your work what your best path is. And make yourself the A Player in that segment. Don't worry, you can always change directions three to five years down the road. Life is long; so is your career. And you'll shift and change as your circumstances shift and change. As I've said before in this book, there are very few career decisions that you can't modify along the way. You just have to do it planfully.

Have a Plan B. Let's say you're passionate about staffing. That's a truly rewarding specialty. It's about growth, creative solutions, fresh beginnings. In the mid- to late-1990s staffing was a great specialty to have. But it wasn't so great at the turn of the century, when companies were downsizing in huge clumps or disappearing altogether. Staffing specialists without a Plan B found themselves downsized out of work themselves.

Pursue your passion but have a fall-back position. If you find yourself especially attracted to specific specialties, consider what economic conditions those specialties would be in particular demand in, and then identify at least one or two specialties in the reverse market that would be almost as compelling for you. Consider it to be like what my co-author, Martha Finney, calls a "career color wheel." For every color, there is a "complementary" color on the opposite side of the chart, for contrast, balance, and appeal. Imagine what the complementary career specialty might be to your passion, and make sure you're proficient in it. For example, great recruiters have excellent sales skills, which would make them a natural in other areas where companies are marketing their products or services to HR functions. Likewise, they have had plenty of experience as career counselors. So why not move over to outplacement?

Make sure you're current on workplace and industry issues. You can't control the emerging HR issues of our time, whether it's immigration, drug testing, or health care. But you can control your knowledge of them. If it's an area that's difficult for you, get the training that you need, read books, network with other professionals who have had experience in these areas, or attend workshops on the matter. One top HR executive once told me that her CEO expected every company executive to spend at least two hours every week reading industry press. If they weren't keeping up with the industry news and trends, their value to the company was quickly diminished. Even if your senior executives don't require this in your organization, this is an excellent passion test. If you're not motivated to stay current on issues that are related either to HR or to your industry, you might consider that an indicator that you should seek out a field or sector that is more compelling for you.

What Every Leadership-Bound Résumé Should Have

When I review résumés in search of high-potential candidates, I look for the following:

- Progressive career growth showing reasonable stability.
- Specific evidence and examples of how the candidate contributed to the business.
- Dedication to overall career growth and professional development. This would include lists of speeches you've made, articles that you've published, professional certifications that you hold, or classes you have taken to upgrade your skills.
- Dedication to the community. Are you involved in some sort of nonprofit work designed to promote your community's future? Are you a mentor? Do you teach or speak at a local high school, community college, or university? Do you help underprivileged populations learn job interviewing skills or work practices to help ensure their success?

Leadership-bound candidates know that HR is more than just a job or even a career. In this profession you can contribute your talents to make the company an important employer and your community a better place. And the beauty of it is this: You can start any time in your career. You don't have to wait until you have "arrived" in order to give back.

WHAT YOU CAN'T CHANGE OVERNIGHT

There are some aspects of your résumé and desirability that you may not be able to change—at least not overnight, if ever.

YOUR PAST. You can't change your past, but you can fix it. It may just take a little time. Try to displace whatever aspects of your past that you consider detrimental to your future prospects with new details that are positive, forward-thinking, productive, and irresistible. It may require a drastic change, like a geographic relocation to a place where no one knows you. Or you may have to jump industry sectors. Or you may choose to leave HR altogether and build your career in a different profession or perhaps as a service provider to HR.

Some black marks on your record will change only with the passage of time—for instance, a rapid succession of job hopping can be changed by a series of three- to five-year stints indicating solid performance and stability in great companies. But some black marks may make it impossible for a recruiter to help you (such as jail time or a record of financial misdoings). That doesn't mean you're out of the game entirely, but you will probably have to network for new positions independent of any extra assistance from recruiting companies.

Your past is going to require your own vigilance and scrutiny. Unless you really solicit feedback from your friends and colleagues, it's unlikely that anyone is going to volunteer the information that your behavior or reputation is holding you back from fulfilling your potential and realizing your dreams. Recruiters certainly won't. They may tell you that you have a spot on your tie, but they won't tell you that you have a smudge on your record.

THE REPUTATION OF YOUR COMPANY. You certainly can't change or control your company's reputation, but you can overcome it as far as your own association with the company is concerned. If your name is attached to a company's malfeasance, you will be linked with the company's behavior for a very long time. The higher up you are in the company, the more intrinsically connected your name will be to the company's reputation in the court of public opinion.

Assuming you had nothing to do with the company's misdeeds, extricate yourself from the organization as quickly as possible. Get a new job before the media catches wind of the gruesome details. Give yourself the luxury of being able to say, "That was after my time," when people notice the name of the company and start probing for juicy bits of information.

Of course, if the reputation is about to take a fall because of illegal activity, your obligation may first be in the service of justice. If you find yourself over your head in this way, your first visit should be to a qualified attorney.

You do have more control over your career than you think you do. The power is always in your hands. This does not mean, necessarily, that your choice will be without a short-term price. But the long-term reward, as you look back over your entire career, will be your ability to tell the story of how you transformed yourself into an A Player—at least in terms of all the values and variables that are the most important to you.

SUMMARY

- Regardless of what details may seem to be getting in your way, you still have control over your career and where your future will take you.
- Identify the characteristics that make up the A Player and A Company in your world, and take the steps necessary to be a player in that arena.
- Have a Plan B to ensure that you're always competitive in any economic environment.
- Know what you can control now, know what you can't control overnight, know what you can never control. And then let it go.

INTERVIEW

Audrey Boone Tillman

Senior Vice President and Director, Human Resources, AFLAC

FOR MOST of her early career, Audrey Tillman thought that she would spend her life developing her promising start in law. Before she joined AFLAC, she had completed a clerkship for a federal district judge and later worked in private practice. She also served as an assistant professor at North Carolina Central University School of Law. When she joined AFLAC, it was the legal department that she joined.

Her big career shift came when AFLAC CEO and Chairman Daniel P. Amos personally asked her to head the HR department of the 6,000-employee company. In this interview she talks about the challenges of making the leap of faith while jumping from one highly specialized function to being the head of another.

What is the best piece of advice you have ever received?

Look at every project as an opportunity to perform with excellence. And I've tried not to take on anything that I didn't feel I would be able to give my best to.

How do you manage to do that and still take on stretch assignments, like leaping from the legal profession to human resources?

That was a tough one. Making that move has been my biggest challenge to date. I can't say that I was dragged into HR kicking and screaming. But I will say that I went into it with one eye opened and the other eye squinted.

I was in the legal division at AFLAC, and I loved my job there. I was vice president, doing very well, highly compensated, all those things. I had no desire whatsoever to leave the legal division. When the opportunity was presented to me by the CEO and our executive vice president, to whom I now report, I just didn't really want to do it. It would have meant a huge promotion for me and a move that a lot of people would have accepted right on the spot. But I asked for time to think about it. I joked that our CEO has a black belt in sales. He called me every day, promising: "I would not leave you hanging. I'll support you. It's a good fit." I trusted him.

I believe strongly in balance. I have a husband and children whom I love. And they are first in my life. When I was presented with this opportunity, my overwhelming concern was my family. I had carved out a nice work-life balance situation for myself in legal and I did not want to do anything that would impact them. Secondly, I didn't know how to run an organization. I just knew how to be a lawyer and how to relate to people.

Then one day I shared my concern with someone about the balance issue. And he said, "Because you're so concerned about that, it lets me know that you should be in HR."

The light bulb went off for me when he said that. I said, "You're right, this is the kind of thing the head of HR would do: Set the corporate tone for issues like this." So I took the position. But I left the back door open. I had an agreement with our general counsel, who was my boss, that if I had to I could come back. He said he'd be glad to take me. Fortunately, I never had to take him up on that promise.

What do you think is important for a non-HR careerist to do to prepare to take on the top spot of the profession?

The first two weeks I was here, the only thing I did was meet individually with every person in this division. I wanted to see what was on their minds and hear their ideas. And we quickly implemented some of those ideas. But my main goal was simply to know more about the people in the division. There were some people who sat down in that chair, and from the minute they sat down to the minute they left, they complained and griped. That told me a lot about them. There were others who had excellent ideas and desperately wanted an audience with the person in my chair. I very much appreciated that.

I also wanted each person to explain to me in his or her own words what he or she did on the job. I told the entire division on my first day there, "I am not ashamed to ask stupid questions. I'm a bright person and a pretty quick study. So bear with me. I'm going to ask you some things you may think are very routine. But I'm not going to ask anything unless I really need to know. So help me understand." And I think that because I took my guard down it broke down a lot of barriers right there.

Didn't you also schedule meetings with HR leaders around the country?

I'm pretty innovative, but there were already answers to most of my questions, and there were people who are already doing things the way I need to do them. So I'm going to learn from them! I don't mind tweaking it and making it my own. I have no shame about exposing what I don't know or learning from people who might be doing things better.

I tried to visit with as many people in my position as possible. I went to conferences that would assemble HR leaders. I still do that once or twice a year. I got one great piece of advice from Coleman Peterson, executive vice president of HR from Wal-Mart. He said, "I hired someone just like you out of legal. I'm going to tell you what I told her: 'Stop being a lawyer. You're not a lawyer anymore.'"

That hit me like a ton of bricks. I was still looking at a lot of decisions through the lenses of a lawyer. And I have a replacement in legal who they hired to do the job I used to do. But I still found myself too involved in that, and I have tried to stop from that day on. You can't imagine how hard it was. There are even times now when I don't agree 100 percent on how something is being handled legally. I voice my opinion, and then I get out of it. That's not my charge anymore.

I realized how difficult it was for my replacement to come and give me a briefing on a legal issue knowing I'd be all over it. I put myself in my replacement's position and backed off. I'm focused now on running the division. And let me tell you, that's plenty.

Do you find the HR community in general embraces newcomers and is generous with its advice and guidance?

Over all, I do! Except there are a few exceptions. I was at a senior HR officer's conference in Philadelphia a couple of years ago and sat at one of those eight-person tables. At our table, six were not career HR people. So we had a lot in common. During the meeting, one guy in the room stood up and said, "One of the problems with what's going on with HR in corporate America is that all these non-HR people are coming into the top roles." We looked at each other and snickered.

As HR gets more integrated with the business side of the enterprise, you're going to find more and more nontraditional HR people in the top roles. You're going to find a lot of people like me who didn't graduate with a degree in human resource management and work their way up.

Don't get me wrong. There is tremendous value in having someone head an HR organization who is trained in HR, has worked in HR for years, and who has taken the traditional route. But I do not think that excludes non-HR people from coming in and heading HR—*provided* they are willing to learn from their staff and learn the area.

What's the one thing you wish you had done differently?

I wish my initial way of thinking had been different. Even though the legal department isn't that involved in the business of the company, I considered what I was working on in legal to be the "hard" issues, the "tough" issues. And I didn't expect that coming to HR would continue that. I felt that I wouldn't be at "the table." What I found was precisely the opposite. I know more about the company's business working in HR. I interact with senior management so much more than I ever in a million years would have in legal. I work on the toughest of the tough issues and many more strategic things. My way of thinking about how things worked was wrong and I found that out very quickly.

What's the best piece of advice you have to offer those on the way up?

Look at every project as an opportunity to work with excellence. I'm very, very anti self-promotion. If anyone wants to get on my bad side, all he has to do is start self-promoting. But I love to see someone's work speak for her. When you work with excellence, you don't have to self-promote. In a company like ours, if you do excellent work and have an excellent attitude, you will do well. You will be recognized. Even though we're Fortune 200, we're still that small. You will be recognized, and you won't need to shine the light on yourself.

Take on one major project each year—something that challenges you. Do a little more than what comes across your plate naturally every day.

What do up-and-coming HR professionals need now that you didn't need back in August 2001 when you started your HR career?

Ambitious HR professionals should learn as much as they can about all areas of HR and become informal generalists. We are customer service people. From an employee's perspective, nothing is worse than calling up a customer service person and getting, "I don't know the answer to that; let me transfer you." The more we can learn about the other areas, the better our customers are going to be served—and the more knowledge you're going to have and the more opportunity you might have to move up when there's an opening in that area. Get out of your cubbyhole. That would be good advice.

What is the best thing new entrants can do for themselves?

Learn your area, but learn and spend time in other parts of the HR department. Nothing would make me happier than to have someone I hired for one area, risk management, for example, say on a light day, "I'm going to call the manager in benefits and see if I can help out over there this afternoon." Or, "I'm going to call the trainers and see if there's a class I can sit in on and watch them teach." I know every area doesn't have the opportunity for that. Some of my areas work non-stop all day. But when there are opportunities for that kind of thing, get out there and learn as many areas as you can.

What is the worst thing they can do?

Not understand their purpose—in the case of AFLAC, to not understand that they are here 100 percent exclusively to support our employees and to help make the employees' jobs and lives easier. If they don't get that, if they don't come in with a customer service attitude, they're not going to make it here. AFLAC is one of *Fortune*'s 100 Best Places to Work and, obviously, an employer of choice. I tell my department that HR should be the best place inside AFLAC to work! We should be the best place in this entire company. We should set the model for what it's like to work at AFLAC.

What risk did you take in your career that paid off?

It was a risk to go from legal to HR. I might have failed miserably. I did it with a lot of help from a lot of people. It did pay off. I'm happy here. I love my staff. There are some challenges. It's not wonderful every single day. But these folks not only care about our employees, they also care about each other.

What is it about the legal profession that you miss now that you're in HR?

Sometimes I really miss the total focus on the work—just being able to come in and do what's been designated as that day's work. In HR, you're dealing by and large with people, not things. And some days I'll sit down to do what I think is my day's work, get interrupted, and not get back to it until a week later. That rarely happens in legal. You have much more control over your day, your week, your month even.

HR is where the rubber meets the road.

7

THE INTERVIEW PROCESS

How to Handle the Hot Seat

As you progress through your career, the environment surrounding the actual interview process will change. You will be dealing with recruiters, search committees, and senior executives of the hiring company—even board members. This chapter ushers you through the various levels of the interview experience and the increasingly sophisticated nature of the interview itself so that you will be prepared for the unexpected.

TO MOST PEOPLE, the interview process is full of tension and anxiety. Their future is at stake, and if they're rejected it's hard not to take it very personally. You understand that. As an HR professional you may have interviewed many job candidates under consideration for positions in your company. It can be stressful, even for you. You may feel how badly some people want the opportunity that's open, and it's painful for you to have to choose one, rejecting the others.

And being the *candidate* interviewing for HR positions is even worse! When you are on that particular hot seat, there's more at stake than merely winning or losing the opportunity that's before you. You're actually demonstrating your professionalism—and your mastery of all the elements that go into it—merely by being a participant in the interview process. Even though you are only a candidate, you are actually performing right there for your peers and colleagues to observe and judge. You are revealing the very level of your professionalism and HR competency by the way you handle your side of the interview process.

To most people, the interview process is just about finding the next job. But for HR professionals, the interview process itself is a key component to building their careers. It's about more than just the job *du jour.* It's about building additional relationships. It's about meeting with your colleagues and peers—some of whom you may already know personally and through various networking activities—in a super-charged environment where much is at stake (how's *that* for pressure to not take final decisions personally?). It's about further cultivating your reputation among your various markets (professional, geographic, and industry-wide, if you are also attached to the sector in which you practice HR). And it's about managing conversations with people whom you yourself may someday recruit into new companies in the future. Or even worse, people you might have interviewed in the past, only to reject them to hire someone else. And now, gulp, here they are again—this time considering *you* as a candidate.

My, my, my, it's a small world, isn't it? And it never feels smaller than when you are interviewing for a position you truly desire. The only way you can emerge from such an experience is to keep it in perspective and to remember that you're a professional practiced in this very setting and process.

Because the generic how-to-find-a-job books tell you everything you need to know about acing an interview, I'm assuming that you already know the basics. At this point in your career, in fact, I'm assuming you're telling others the basics. Consequently, this chapter is not about using the interview process to "find a job"; it's about taking your professional experience to the next level, perhaps into unfamiliar territory where the conventions might be a little different. And instead of focusing only on landing a job, what I'll be talking to you about in this chapter is how to use the interview process to continue building your career and relationships, regardless of whether you are offered this particular position.

At this level of your professional awareness, it should be obvious to you that the search and interview processes have value that extends well beyond the simple task at hand of landing the next job. And if you bear that principle in mind, it might take the pressure off the question: Will you or won't you be offered this job? Well, maybe at least a little bit.

If you have come this far in this book, you have already identified yourself as *leadership-bound.* You have progressed through your first HR positions (or expect to some time very soon). And you are ready to leverage your experiences and contacts to help you progress to the next levels of your career. You have found a way to come to the current job market "pre-approved." You have an established track record of success. People know you and are saying good things about you. You have been building and filling your career kit over time.

This may mean that you have been on the HR scene for a year, maybe three, maybe five, maybe even more. But the key here is that your basic skills, abilities, and experiences are assumed. You have now graduated to a new realm of recruiting in which you will be talking to more senior recruiters—even groups of interviewers—internal or external, all of whom want to know not *what* you can do, but *how well* you can do it, that is, how you can creatively apply the principles you've learned so far and how effectively you can link your experiences and responsibilities to the overall business concern and strategy, and how you can use your abilities to move the new company toward its own objectives.

HOW THE INTERVIEW ENVIRONMENT CHANGES

As you leave the entry-level interview process behind, you'll notice significant changes in the nature of the interviews themselves. The environment shifts noticeably, very much like going from true/false and multiple choice questions on a test to essay questions. And this is appropriate. As the complexity of your work evolves, you must be able to converse about your contributions and ideas more and more. Proving that you have the skills will become less and less important. It will just be assumed that you do.

The higher the level of the open opportunity, the more complex the interviewing process is going to be: More people involved, greater depth of questions, and more time you can expect to spend interviewing to finally arrive at that final offer. The other rule of thumb is that who will be on that committee of interviewees will depend on the nature of the position that's open. Some examples are discussed below.

HR REP, ANALYST, OR ENTRY-LEVEL GENERALIST POSITION. You can probably expect a phone screening by a recruiter (at this level, the recruiter is usually someone within the company or someone from an agency working on behalf of the company) and/or the hiring authority. Assuming you pass the phone screen, the second step would be a personal interview in which you'll be brought in to meet the hiring authority, perhaps a company recruiter, a few peers, and possibly the hiring authority's boss. What's critical at this level is that you prepare for the phone interview. If you don't get past this stage, no one gets to see you. You need to be able to show energy, enthusiasm, and passion over the phone. Phone screeners can't see body language. All they hear is your voice. If your voice doesn't reflect your energy and passion about your work, you may not get to the next step.

A SENIOR GENERALIST ROLE. This is a senior professional position, but not an executive- (or management-) level role. In addition to the usual phone screening, you could easily be meeting six to ten people during the interview process, more often than not in one-on-one settings (although a few companies do panel interviews). Expect to meet the hiring authority (the person to whom this position reports directly, probably the HR director or division vice president of HR). You'll also meet people in peer positions, because you'll be working closely and collaboratively with them, and they want to make sure you can work well together. There will probably be some representatives from specialty areas, such as staffing, compensation, organization development, and training. Since you would probably be supporting a line group, expect to meet a line manager or two.

THE HEAD OF A SPECIALTY AREA. Again, after at least one successful phone screening, you would meet the hiring authority, who is usually the vice president of HR and your peers (the heads of other specialty areas in this case). You can also expect to talk with the people you'd be providing services directly to—such as the line managers you would be supporting and the HR generalists you'd be collaborating with.

THE CHIEF VICE PRESIDENT LEVEL. Again, you can expect to speak with the hiring authority, the person you would be working directly for. Only in this case it would be the CEO. Your peers will also want to meet you: The top vice presidents of sales, engineering, manufacturing, and so on. You should also expect to meet with a board member or two, since the HR vice president is expected to advise the board on the ramifications of its decisions and actions on employees. The HR vice president may also have to interact with the board on issues such as succession plans, executive compensation plans, and other even more sensitive matters, so board members will want to make sure there is chemistry, trust, and respect between you and them.

•

Interview Questions Top Executives Are Asked

If you have progressed through your first couple of jobs already, you may have noticed that interview questions tend to evolve and become more complex with the additional experience and responsibility the open position requires. Eventually, your grade point average, for instance, is no longer so important. You'll notice that no one is as interested in what software programs you're competent in.

More complex professional levels require more complex interview questions, which, in turn, require more complex answers and a seasoned understanding of how exactly your profession plays into the overall prospects of the company. Here are examples of interview questions top HR executives are asked. You may not necessarily be asked these questions word for word. But if you go into an interview with the answers to these questions or requests, you'll be better prepared for whatever questions they surprise you with:

- "Tell us about how you were a factor in a successful initiative in your previous company. What was the initial objective? What made it succeed? What were your contributions to its success?"
- "We are facing a particular business problem in the near future. Here are the key factors. And this is our objective. How would you go about helping us achieve that objective?"
- "What was the most complex work you've ever done?"
- "How did you *approach* key people issues and problems in your previous company?"
- "What was the most sensitive political problem or cross-functional project you worked on? How did you come to understand its variables? And how did you resolve the problem?"

Keep in mind that these questions will contain valuable information for you. If you listen very carefully to the kinds of questions the search committee will be asking, you will get significant insight into what to expect in the job itself. Listen for an extra emphasis on a particular kind of problem: politics, staffing, accounting, a CEO on a power trip. You may find everything you need to learn will be there, buried in those questions.

•

Aside from the different make-up and functional levels of these hiring groups—in some cases formally convened search committees—the actual processes will be similar. The spirit of these interviews should be one of mutual discovery. Naturally, to be realistic, since you're the candidate meeting them on their home turf, you may feel as though they hold the power. But not only are they interviewing you, you're also interviewing them. This is your opportunity to find out all you can about the company, its culture, and its opportunity before you make the decision to accept the job. Even though you may feel as though you're the one on stage, feeling the heat of the scrutinizing spotlight, they're also on stage.

And the more extraordinary your qualifications are, or the tighter the employment market, the more invested they're feeling in making sure you leave with a positive impression of the opportunity they've laid before you.

HOW WILL THE INTERVIEWS VARY?

As you move into ever-higher levels of interviews and opportunities, the nature of the interview conversation will also move into higher levels of discussion. Interviewers are going to be increasingly interested in how what you have done has served the interests of the business as a whole—not just the tactical needs of HR itself. The pressure is on how not only to deliver scintillating examples of what you have done, but to also link it to what matters most from the perspective of your interviewers: How can you help them meet their goals and objectives? And you must be prepared to make those links for them.

Typically, organizations work off of models based on behavioral interviewing techniques. The belief is that the best predictor of future performance is past performance. And so they will ask you to describe a situation or tell a story. They're going to be looking for specifics about the work you've done in terms of business outcomes, in clearly defined terms:

- What was the problem and how did you solve it?
- What did you do that had an impact and for whom?
- And how did you go about it?

If you're interviewing for an employee relations position, for example, they may ask what the most common employee relations problem that you handled was, or what the most *complex* problem that you had to handle was. Tell a story about a particular situation—a harassment investigation or wrongful termination situation, for instance. (This is where your career journal will come in very handy. The night before the interview, re-familiarize yourself with the highlights from your résumé and career journal. You may already have "handled complex employee relations problems" on your résumé, but with the prompting of your career journal, you will be able to go into the interview equipped to tell the stories behind that résumé line item: What happened. How you handled it. The complexities. And the outcomes.)

They're going to want to know: Do you really know your stuff? Your story can even have a bad outcome. You didn't create the problem, after all; you were only chartered with *resolving* the problem. The story you are telling—no matter what the outcome was—is how you tried to solve the problem in the best possible way, minimizing the costs and risks to the company and, one hopes, having everyone get on with their lives somehow. What they will look for in the interview is not necessarily a happy ending but the answer to their question: "What was his process for solving the problem and how well did he handle it?"

(It's possible that a story with a good outcome could work against you, particularly if it reveals your lack of knowledge in the subject area. In HR, there are some basic norms that can't be violated. I've had candidates go through a story where they violated many norms because they didn't have the proper training. What the interviewers will be looking for is not only what you did but *how* you did it. They want to make sure that when you come aboard, you will be equipped with the proper training to get the job done right.)

Interviewers will also want to know what you learned from your experiences, even (or especially) the bad ones. Expect to be asked: "If you had it to do over again, is there anything you would have done differently? What might that be?" You may have gone through the best possible process and come out with just an okay outcome. But if you realize in hindsight that "If I had done something just a little bit differently, I would have come out with a better outcome," well, then, you may be a high-potential candidate with a demonstrated capacity to learn and add value to the company in future years.

A sign for the hiring committee that you are a seasoned, mature professional is that you take the philosophy that not every HR action is going to come out wonderfully. They know they don't all come out perfectly. They've been there themselves. Again, HR does not create the problems. One of the reasons why HR exists in the company is to solve the problems that naturally come about in work environments when you mix a lot of different people into a building doing a lot of different things. And so you have to expect problems to occur, and you have to do the best job that you can, using the best processes and knowledge that you can to solve them—and then learn from the experience.

No one is expecting you to be perfect. In fact, wise search committees know that the opposite is the case. If you haven't made mistakes you probably haven't been growing. They might even ask you about the worst mistake you've ever made and what you did about it. With the mistake question, what they want to see is how you recovered. The recovery is just as important if not more so than doing it right to begin with.

When you get higher into the executive levels, they're going to ask many more questions around the business itself. How much do you know about the business you're in? They're going to ask about the market. They're going to ask why your company is successful or why it's not. They expect you to know a bit about that. They'll expect you to know about product plans and marketing plans. Of course, they won't expect you to disclose things that are confidential, especially if you're talking with a competitor. But they will be listening for a sense of fluency in the way you're able to talk about overall business issues. What do you know about the business you're in? Do you even know what your company's product is and what it does?

If you're working for a company that produces drugs that treat or cure cancer, it's really easy to get close to the product because everyone has a personal attachment. It hits home. But if you're working for a company that makes some sort of electronic box that goes into another piece of equipment, it's hard to feel any real affection for it. Take computer chips, for example. What does your chip do? Even with this kind of product, you have to be able to show interest in and knowledge about the industry and where your company stands in that market.

DO YOU UNDERSTAND THE BUSINESS?

Can you read a profit and loss (P&L) statement? Somewhere you have to obtain that business knowledge, whether it's in your undergraduate days studying to be in human resources or later in some night courses. You can't fake this kind of understanding, and you can't expect to go far in HR today without it. When you make a recommendation to a company to take some kind of action, you have to understand what the impact is going to be on the organization, the culture, and the P&L. What those executives care about is the P&L. Some things in HR are hard to quantify, but you have to be able to quantify as much as you can.

The higher up you go in the organizational interviewing process, the more your interviewers will want to know what you can do for them in the future. They will want to know that you not only understand business in general, but that you also understand *their* business. You can only base your response on information you have acquired through your research and the interviews so far. Step delicately around these kinds of answers. You want to sound thoughtful, creative, and solution-oriented, but you don't want to sound arrogant or critical. For example, you might say, "Based on what you've shared with me, I believe that you feel your biggest problem is . . . . I think there are a number of ways I might be able to contribute . . . ." And then list them. Or tell a story that reflects potential solutions: "When I was in XYZ company we faced a similar issue. We took this approach . . . , which was effective there. It may or may not be effective here, but there were certainly some lessons I learned there that will help me be successful in helping you accomplish your objective."

You want to play off what you've done and what their key issues are. Their key issue may be "Our HR department is a mess and we need someone to come in and clean it up." But you naturally wouldn't go into a company and say, "I think your HR department is a mess and I want to come in and fix it for you."

But if you're able to identify specifics that indicate how it is that the HR department is a "mess," focus on those and the experiences you have had in the past that might be borrowed to remedy the situation. "What you've told me is that you feel there is still work to be done in HR, and that you would like to take it to the next level. I think that what I could do for you is . . . ." You don't want to be presumptuous. You don't want to assume that someone else did a bad job and you can come in and fix it. Keep the conversation positive.

DO YOU UNDERSTAND YOUR OWN CAREER PATH?

I find interviewers increasingly wanting to know what kind of future you see for yourself and how you are laying out your career plans. Even if you just fell into HR, it's essential to be able to speak of the future of your career in more planful terms. Be the agent of your own fortune and future.

Be able to talk about how you have gone about developing your career so far and why. Where do you see it going? You should at least work out a direction in your mind. You want to be able to say that you're looking for roles where you can continue to learn and that will prepare you for the future. It's okay to tell them, "I want to be a really well-rounded HR professional so that one day I could qualify to be in your job. I think that a couple of things need to happen for me to prepare myself for that. I want to work for a great HR vice president whom I can learn from."

Don't feel as though you must inflate your own ambitions simply because you think that's what the search committee wants to hear. Not everyone wants to be vice president of HR, and not every search committee is looking for a candidate who is on that track. I have seen a number of candidates who have told me, "I am a really great Number Two person. That's what I want to do. This is my love, this is my passion."

And that's okay. I know many HR vice presidents who are looking for you. Whatever it is that you want to do, however high you want to climb in business, be sure you can speak passionately and authentically about your career and what it is you want to do. There are plenty of things you can be passionate about.

THEY'LL BE JUDGING YOU ON THE QUESTIONS *YOU* ASK

I've had candidates eliminated because they didn't ask good questions or because they asked no questions at all! Keep in mind that in these elevated interview scenarios, this is your chance to evaluate the possibilities laid out before you, just as it's their opportunity to consider you as a candidate for the open role. If you don't take an active, equal part in this process of mutual discovery, it's possible that you will be seen as being too junior for the position in question. So you need to be able to ask good questions, such as:

- What are the business challenges facing the company?
- How do you think HR might be able to help?
- Where do you see the company stacking up against the competition today? How do you see that changing?

Make sure your questions are customized specifically to the roles of the individuals you're speaking with. If you're talking with the CEO, for instance, ask about his or her vision for the company. How is the company growing and evolving into the future? What are the biggest challenges as perceived from the highest office? What does he or she see as being the biggest people challenges? What would he or she like to see from HR? What does success in HR look like at the end of the day, end of the quarter, end of the year?

If you're speaking with a leader of a line organization and you're interviewing for an HR generalist slot, these questions may be more appropriate:

- What are the toughest business issues you face in your organization? (Don't limit the context of the question only to what they perceive as people issues. As the HR expert, you can make legitimate connections to other issues that may not be obviously people-oriented to non-HR professionals.)
- To what do you attribute your organization's success?
- What do you consider to be the greatest risk to your continued success?

- What do you think of the HR services you've been receiving thus far?
- What would you like to see more of?
- What would you like to see less of?
- What do you think HR could be doing better to help you run your business and be more successful? (Expect the line management to regard HR in terms of the services it provides.)

As you are noting their wish list, they're also giving you valuable insight into how to hit the ground running when you begin the job. When you ask these kinds of questions, you are receiving in return a list of high-value successes that you can accomplish immediately—thereby solidifying your place inside the new company and building your new network of raving fans.

Even if you receive a hostile response from line managers, take *that* as valuable information. Here's a difference you can make inside the company—if you are interested in achieving that shift. Maybe they've never worked with a great HR person before so they don't understand the value. You could change that. What you do works across the organization and across everyone's boundaries. You want to know how they feel about HR, what their expectations are, and what they're ready for and not ready for. That might affect your decision. Maybe the answers to your questions reveal that this is not a job you want to take. This is valuable information in and of itself. Maybe you're not at a stage in life where you need or want to prove the value of HR.

You should also ask about your predecessor: "Is this a newly created position, or are you seeking a replacement?" If they are seeking a replacement, where did the last individual go and why? Don't necessarily expect to get a straight answer on that last question, especially if that person left under a cloud. Do you have the feeling that there is something seriously negative that is going unsaid? If you have serious concerns about the background of the company or its history with HR, frame that concern into a question and then ask that question of a number of different people. It may be something or it may be nothing. As you work through the interview process, it will become more clear.

•

Essential Questions You Must Ask Recruiters

When you're contacted by an executive recruiter, it's normal to feel that the burden is on you to make the best impression and "pass inspection" in order to move on to the client company. No wonder you might feel nervous and at something of a disadvantage. But you are just as much in a power seat as the recruiter is. And when you keep that in mind, you position yourself to be considered for the opportunities that are most suitable for you and your ambitions.

Think of the initial recruiter meeting as a screening opportunity for both of you. Sure, you must still impress the recruiter so he or she will decide to put you in the pool of qualified candidates. But if you ask these questions, you will decide whether this particular opportunity is something that *you* want to pursue:

- What is the nature of the position? Who does it report to? Why is the position open? How is HR perceived in the company?
- What is the culture and environment of the organization? What kinds of people are successful there?
- What is the salary range? (Make sure that the company's budget for this position falls within your expectations. If it's not an increase that is sufficiently attractive to you to entice you to leave your current position, it's better to know that now. Being honest with your recruiter from the very beginning may disqualify you for the position at hand, but the recruiter may remember you for a similar, but better-paying position. Since the recruiter will eventually negotiate on your behalf, should the interview process result in an offer, it's even more essential that she or he knows what your expectations are from the very beginning.)

Finally, at the conclusion of your interview with the recruiter, find out how well you did in the interview process itself. Does he or she have any suggestions on your appearance or demeanor? You can also ask for specific coaching on what aspects of your experience you should emphasize when the time comes for you to interview with the company itself.

The recruiter interview is a valuable fact-finding opportunity for you! Use it for all it's worth!

THE FINE POINTS OF MANAGING YOUR INTERVIEW

Be yourself, but don't make the mistake of confusing your genuine personality with being too relaxed. I had one candidate who came very close to losing a dream job because she forgot where she was and what she was there for. The interview process was so enjoyable for everyone concerned that she had the job in the palm of her hand before she left the building. But she didn't know it, and she also didn't know she lost it just as certainly when she uttered four little words on her way out: "I have to pee."

It's still unbelievable that she would say such a thing, even as these words are being typed! But such is the drawback of a relaxed, spontaneous candidate. Unfortunately (and certainly understandably), the client company perceived that slip as a sign that she lacked polish and, in their own minds, withdrew their intention to offer her the job. She almost never found out.

The client company then went through a number of other candidates, searching for someone who matched—or surpassed—this candidate's competencies, but didn't find anyone whose skills exceeded hers. So I urged them to give this candidate another try. After all, everyone commits a *faux pas* every now and then.

Before she went in for her second interview, I called her. As gently as I could, I coached her to be careful what she said and how she said it. And I told her specifically why. She took the advice in the spirit in which I offered it to her. Then she went in for the second interview and landed the job.

When you finish your round of interviews, make sure you close with the primary hiring authority and the recruiter. Ask them, "What should I anticipate the next step being?" It's a nice, open question and you deserve to know what to expect. After all, you're a busy person, and you gave them your time as much as they gave you theirs. You'll probably hear a response such as, "We have several other candidates to talk to. Once we go through that process, you should be hearing back from us." You say: "Great. Is there an anticipated timeframe for that?" Keep it soft, light, unstressful. And now you have a date to put on your calendar for following up.

You'll probably be called in for second or third rounds of interviews. I've seen as many as six or eight rounds. It's not necessarily a bad sign. It could just signify that there is a lot of organizational change or that this is a very important hire for the company. It's a nuisance. But it's not uncommon.

Take rejection in stride. Not every candidate is perfect for every job. You're perfect for many jobs, I'm sure, but maybe not the one that's open at the moment. Be philosophical about it and use the rejection (if you can even call it that) as another way to demonstrate your professionalism.

I had a candidate once who was a thoroughly qualified compensation expert. However, this candidate was missing some significant, but seemingly minor (at least to him) skills that the client company specifically requested. So I had to break the news to him that, despite his expertise, he would not be progressing through the company interview process. To say he blew his top puts it mildly. He yelled at me, criticizing my judgment. And then he simply said, "Well, I'm just going to go ahead and present myself without you." Keeping my cool, I responded: "Whatever you think is appropriate."

Then I called my client, filling her in on what had just happened and giving her fair warning that this former candidate would be sending his résumé to her directly.

She said: "And when I receive it, I will file it. If you don't think he's qualified, then I'm not interested. And if he doesn't have the good sense to behave more professionally than this, how is he going to behave when things don't go his way if I let him into my organization working with my executive team?"

His candidacy went nowhere. And I'll never approach him with another opportunity. We just won't call him for positions we're working on. I don't want to deal with his behavior, and I really don't want my clients to have to deal with his behavior either.

Of course, this is extraordinarily rare. What generally happens is that candidates respond with, "Thank you. This isn't the outcome I was hoping for, but you were very gracious for calling me and telling me." These candidates will be contacted again as new opportunities present themselves.

Solicit feedback. Even though the hiring company is the recruiter's paying client, you can use the recruiter as a coach. You never know how you're coming across to others unless someone tells you. You can still be yourself. With feedback you'll have the additional support of knowing that you may be unconsciously doing or saying things that don't put you in the best light. And feedback from trusted sources will also help you refine your behaviors and actions to a level that is appropriate for the roles you're aspiring to. (Just as you should dress for the job you want, you should also act appropriately for the next job as well.) If you want to be an executive, you need to look like an executive and behave like an executive. Are you trading away some of you? Maybe. But that's a decision only you can make.

Again, ask the recruiter for feedback.

AFTER THE INTERVIEW

Much has changed over recent years of boom and bust, technological advancements, and your own career rise through the various levels of HR. But the basic rules of courtesy have prevailed. What you do after the interview process can have a powerful impact on what happens next.

As it has been for decades, it continues to be important to send a quick thank-you note to people you interview with. Fortunately, technology has made it easier. Email is preferable unless you don't have an email address for your interviewers (get their business cards as part of the routine preliminaries every time you start your meeting with them). Your thank-you messages should be brief, to the point, and somehow customized to mention some detail that came out of the meeting (you can smell a form letter a mile away; so can they). Just a short paragraph thanking them for their time will do the trick. Say something nice about the company and the people you've met. Express your excitement about what you heard about the company and its future. Let them know you're looking forward to the possibility of working with them one day. And, of course, invite them to get back in touch with you if they need further information. Try to resist using that tired expression, "Please don't hesitate to ask." Really. Who ever hesitates?

Resist the temptation to resell or oversell yourself. If you think you've lost the opportunity and you're pretty sure you're not going to get the job, you might want to take a moment to emphasize a positive point that came out of the interview. You have nothing to lose, but it's probably not going to help you either.

Not sending a note, however, could cause you to lose a great opportunity to advance in your career. It's rare, but I've actually had candidates rejected by client companies because the candidates didn't send a thank-you note. The client will tell me, "Great candidate, but he didn't have the common sense to follow up or say thank you. I won't be pursuing this candidate further." It's rare that the client company would go to that extreme, but why take the risk? It's good common courtesy, so take the two minutes and just do it.

MONEY

Money is a tough area for many people—especially these days when, after the boom of the late 1990s, your compensation history may be completely out of kilter with the current market. You may have been making a tremendous amount of money when it was a seller's market, but now you're unemployed and you just want to get back into the game. You're smart, you're a realist, you read *The Wall Street Journal*. You know full well that the chances are slim you'll be able to re-enter at the same financial level you left. But how to convince the search committee that you've accepted that fact?

Or you may be underpaid. And you worry that if you tell the search committee what you make they'll continue to underpay you. Or they won't understand your real value.

All those issues run through people's minds. Be honest and forthright about where your thinking is. If they want your salary history, give them the history. If you have feelings about it that you think are important, feel free to share them. Be matter-of-fact about it, be unemotional. If your well-considered expectations rule you out of consideration for that particular opening, you probably wouldn't have wanted that move anyway.

If you absolutely want the job and don't want to run the risk of losing the opportunity because of salary expectations (too high or too low), put your desires to the search committee (or to the recruiter, if you're working with one) more gently: "I recognize that my salary history is on the higher end of the current market. As long as the company is able to make a reasonable, competitive offer . . . ."

One of two responses will likely come back to you:

- "I really need to know what your history is and what your expectations are," which would be my question if I were screening you as a recruiter; or
- "What do you believe reasonable market pay is?"

They'll want to know where your thinking is. Say something like "Based on the company size and the position, the data I looked at is somewhere around $175k to $200k base, plus bonus and stock." Putting it that way sounds far better than "Based on the fact the economy has gone to hell, I'm willing to take whatever you're willing to offer."

If you have access to data, tell them what the data is. It demonstrates that you're realistic and pragmatic about your career. It also shows that you're systematic and experienced in evaluating compensation and other HR issues. If they want to push for the previous information, go ahead and tell them. Also tell them that if the role is right, the company is right, and the job is right, money is a secondary issue.

If you are prepared to take a drastic cut in pay, for whatever reason, an unspoken concern will be what your financial obligations are from your previous income level and whether you will be stressed about continuing to meet them. While the search committee probably won't broach the subject, it doesn't mean they won't be thinking about it. So you have to be prepared to anticipate their concerns and volunteer a reassurance that you're comfortable with the lower salary: "My life is well set. I've been very fortunate in life, and so money is not my primary motivator. I'm most interested in the scope and the responsibility of the job and the contribution I can make."

As this book is being written, the overall hiring climate is less than optimal. So it's tempting to frame all this advice in the "buyer's market" context. But books have a long shelf life, and I certainly want this book to be useful to you throughout your career and in all economic climates. There could be a time when you can afford to be more aggressive financially about an opportunity that is on the table with your name on it. You're happy where you are. You like your work. You like your income. You're not especially motivated to take a chance and change.

So what might move you from your comfortable position? Let's assume the job *looks* right for you. The company is right. Everything is in place, but it wouldn't necessarily make sense to take the risk to move from a job you're in now to this other job. And other jobs always have unknowns to them. Your existing job has knowns. You know it intimately. The new job may look wonderful, but you're smart enough to realize there may be a couple of unpleasant surprises. You're in great shape now. Why take the risk?

You're in an ideal position to really negotiate from a position of strength at this point. Maybe the right financial package is the thing that would entice you to jump into a new, risky environment.

Even if you're not in the perfect job and you're really interested in this potential position, in better economic times, there is a normal expectation that when you change jobs you will probably get more money for doing so. So in good economic times, companies expect that they will have to entice you from where you are to something new; they will have to add something extra in the package for you to make the move. In those cases, you should get very comfortable with negotiating a compensation package. So when they ask you what your expectations are, be prepared to tell them: "I'm currently at this position. This is my base, my bonus, and my stock. My expectations are that I would be able to do better than this. I would hope it would be consistent with the significant increase in scope and responsibility that this new position represents. And I would expect to be compensated reasonably for that. Based on the data I've been able to accumulate on this position, I believe that it should be in the . . . . . .range." Be matter-of-fact about it. Be comfortable and confident asking.

The only time you should not be comfortable asking for more is if it's critical that you get this job and you don't want to risk losing it. But if you're prepared to not get this job and you're happy being right where you are while you wait to get a better offer, then do it! Negotiate the best offer you can!

THE OFFER PROCESS

If the hiring company is dealing directly with you (without taking the opening to a recruitment agency), you are, unfortunately, on your own in the negotiation process. In normal economic times, a 10 to 15 percent increase in salary wouldn't be unusual. If you and the client company are working with an agency, the recruiter generally negotiates the offer *for* you. Very early in the process, the recruiter should ask you what your compensation is and what your expectations are. As I've already said, this should be an open discussion. If the client doesn't want to pay what you want, they shouldn't be wasting your time sending you through the interview process. As recruiters, we also tell candidates what the client's range is. By the time the entire process comes down to an actual offer, the recruiter has done the advance work to bring the two sides of the process together. And the offer itself is little more than a formality. The remaining task now is mainly just a piece of paper that needs to be signed.

As you progress through the discovery process of the interview cycle, everyone on both sides of the negotiating table should have a firm idea of what to expect. The elements of the offer itself are generally very common:

COMPENSATION AND BENEFITS. Your compensation will be typically made up of base pay, bonus, and stock, especially at the senior levels, all of which could be subject to negotiation. Your recruiter will have a good sense of what is fair in your market area and experience level. If you have access to one or more salary surveys (possibly Towers Perrin, Mercer, Aon, or SHRM, for example), you can check the competitive market data for your region as well.

PERQUISITES. Companies aren't quite as creative as they used to be with the array of extra features that are available for negotiation—especially for lower-level positions. Whatever is available for one person is typically available to some extent for everyone. You or your recruiter might be able to create a more attractive package that includes (in very rare circumstances) additional vacation leave, additional educational or relocation assistance, or a more advantageous bonus scheme. If you are taking an international assignment, you can probably include private English-speaking school tuition for your children and club membership dues for the local American Club where you will be assigned. This is not simply a luxury, as a golf club membership stateside might be. Companies know that families that are happy and well-established while abroad are more likely to have a successful outcome.

If you are taking on a vice president spot in a smaller company or a start-up, you or your recruiter may be able to negotiate a *change of control* agreement. Because high-quality small companies and start-ups are subject to being acquired, your own job security is at risk in the acquisition. So you may be able to obtain some form of protection for yourself in the form of severance pay or stock vesting, for example.

COUNTEROFFERS

I'll put it as simply and as plainly as possible: Don't entertain counteroffers. This holds true whether or not you're working with a professional recruiter. If you have progressed all the way to the offer stage with the hiring company, you should also, by that time, be committed to leaving your current company. Whatever your original reasons for deciding to leave your present employer may have been, those reasons are still valid, no matter how much money they promise you to entice you to stay. You may have outgrown your boss or your job. You may find you need to work in a company whose industry has better prospects. Perhaps you want a more people-friendly or more HR-friendly environment. You don't really expect those burning issues to go away just because your original employer has fattened your paycheck, do you?

If you're still not convinced, here's the clincher: Even if your current employer has found a way to entice you to stay a little while longer, in your boss's mind you're already gone. Even though you may be bringing home a larger salary, you may discover that you're no longer factored into long-term plans. After all, who knows when you might consider leaving again? So there's no real bargain to be had by accepting your current company's counteroffer, no matter how sincerely they say they want you to stay.

Accepting your current company's counteroffer is also unfair to the hiring company and the recruiter. If you've interviewed with them to the extent that they're ready to extend an offer, they've already spent many hours on you, interviewing, getting you through the process, checking references, and so forth. In the meantime, they've also passed up other great candidates for you. By accepting the counteroffer, you will have put everyone (including yourself) in a terrible position. So that should be avoided at all costs.

This isn't to say that participating in the search process prematurely commits you to the job even before the offer is made. If you think you might want to stay where you are or you're not sure about the opportunity, you should tell the recruiter about that ahead of time. Also, you can search for other opportunities while you're being actively considered by the hiring company. That's only fair. After all they're considering other candidates up until they commit themselves to you by extending the offer. It's a matter of good faith, honesty, and integrity on all sides. And ultimately, should you take the low road and accept a counteroffer, expect the negative ripple effects of your decision to extend well into the future. The recruiter will recover from the embarrassment. The employer will recover from the disappointment. But you will never know what damage this choice may do to your career well into the future.

I was at a dinner meeting one night, and there were a half dozen vice presidents of HR from major Northern California corporations sitting around the table having a casual conversation before the main meeting began. One of the HR leaders chimed in to say how disappointed she was about a recent experience she had trying to hire a new compensation director. The candidate had accepted the offer and, during the two-week notice period, had come over to corporate headquarters to meet his future team, get personally acquainted, even pick up copies of the company's compensation plans—very sensitive material indeed. The Saturday before the Monday he was supposed to begin, he called the HR leader on her cell phone and told her that he decided not to accept the position after all! He had decided to accept the counteroffer where he was. From his perspective, that might have been the end of it. However, he didn't know what was to happen that very Monday night—the HR leadership dinner meeting in which his story was told.

It goes without saying that that HR vice president will never consider him again as a candidate. However, as a recruiter sitting at the table, I will know never to present him to any of my clients. Those six senior vice presidents of HR represent companies he'll never get to work at either. Will he *ever* recover from that ill-considered Saturday phone call? That's a very good question.

SHOULD YOU "GO FOR THE OFFER," NO MATTER WHAT?

In a word: No. You may hear advice, especially in the early years of your career, to "go for the offer." This means: Bring the hiring manager all the way to the point where he or she extends the offer to you. And then *you* can decide at the last minute whether to take it. Except in the most entry-level phase of your career, when your main objective is to break in (and even then preferably into the best position possible), this level of interviewing is not about landing every offer regardless of whether you want it. Leave the "catch and release" philosophy to fishing.

If you take an employer all the way to the phase in which an offer is extended to you and you say, "No," you risk burning at least one bridge, if not several. As the entire interviewing team (you included) progresses through the various phases of the interview process, everyone has the right to expect and assume that the environment has remained an open and honest one. It's a collaborative process, not a game—especially at the senior levels.

If you take them all the way to an offer, fully expecting to turn them down, it may embarrass everyone concerned. The search committee may feel as though they've been led on; they will have wasted their time cultivating a relationship with the wrong candidate; and they'll have to resort to turning to their Number 2 choice, hoping that he or she won't pick up on the fact that he or she wasn't the first selection. The recruiter, if there is one involved, will be embarrassed because your rejection of the offer will reflect poorly on him or her (your recruiter should always be current with the issues and concerns you may be feeling about the opportunity). And worst of all, you run the risk of leaving a bad feeling behind about you. And you don't want to do that. *Today* it may not be the right fit, right role, right opportunity, or right company. But what about a year or so later? Everything may have changed—except how they remember the way you treated them during this go-round. Who knows? Maybe some of the search committee members themselves will have gone on to the A Player company of your dreams. Oops.

(Or as luck will almost always have it: You're on a search committee one day tasked with the great opportunity of attracting a key contributor. This opportunity is a fabulous moment in your career, and you're proud of the fact that you've been invited to shape your company's future. The résumé you hold before you is perfect. A real plum candidate. You can't wait to meet her. But wait a minute! That name! So familiar. Oh. It's all coming back to you now. Uh oh.)

This doesn't mean to imply that you're 100 percent committed to saying yes all the way to the very end. You may be considering other prospective opportunities (that's only fair; the search committee is talking with more candidates too). And you may have some reservations and apprehensions that the fit may not be the best one for you. That's only natural. You'll come closer to deciding as the discovery process unfolds. That's what the interview process is for.

If you progress through the various stages of conversation and you remain 90 percent sure that the opportunity is an appropriate next step in your career, by all means, go for it. But if you are thinking that there may be a 50 percent chance you're not going to accept the offer, then it's a mistake to take them all the way to that phase without at least giving fair warning.

If you're working with an agency recruiter, that responsibility is a little easier for you. You can be candid with the recruiter without worrying that you would be perceived as personally rejecting the entire company. But even if you must deal with the company directly, a gracious approach will save everyone precious time and leave everyone feeling good about themselves and each other: "You know, I really like everyone personally. I've enjoyed working with you on this search. But after serious thought, I have to conclude that this job is just not right for me at this time. I'm really sorry. I'd love to stay in touch. Maybe at some other point in time we can talk again."

They may still extend an offer to you, hoping that as a group they can neutralize your concerns. But at least you've been up-front and open, letting them know that there is a good chance you won't take the offer because, for whatever reason, you're not comfortable with the role.

Remember: It's not just about landing a new job. Regardless of whether you received an offer or not, you should perceive each round of interviews as an essential part of building your career *over time*. Each round is an opportunity to meet new people, develop your own network of powerful people who know who you are and what you've done, and gain new insights into how HR is managed in yet another company and industry. It's all an opportunity to learn and develop yourself.

And don't think your chances with each company are over just because you might be told "No, thanks." By handling the interview and offer process graciously, even when declining the offer, it is possible to maintain great relationships with the company and the individuals involved. I know of many situations in which the candidate who rejected an offer because the position wasn't quite right (or when the company rejected the candidate) was contacted again later for an opportunity that turned out to be wonderful. In the end, everyone won, both the company and the candidate.

SUMMARY

- As you progress through the ranks in your career, the interview process will change as well. You must be prepared to discuss increasingly sophisticated aspects of business and how HR serves organizational objectives.

- It's not always essential that you know the answers. But you must be able to demonstrate how you would approach problems and issues as they present themselves to your prospective "clients" inside the company.
- Be prepared to tell stories, beginning with the business issue being addressed, of what you have done in the past to illustrate examples of problems that you have solved or contributions you have made for your previous employers.
- Come prepared to *ask* sophisticated questions. You will be judged on the quality of your questions as much as you will be evaluated on your answers to theirs.
- Be prepared to discuss compensation expectations in a professional, unemotional way.
- Relax.

INTERVIEW

Jim Wall

National Managing Director, Human Resources, Deloitte & Touche

AFTER BEGINNING *his professional life in academia, Jim Wall followed his wife into the HR profession. Her relocation to the Boston area from Michigan presented him with the opportunity to explore other career options before continuing with his career in education in any one of Boston's many colleges and universities. After an interview with what would eventually become Deloitte & Touche, Jim made the shift and hasn't looked back.*

In this interview Jim talks about how the attacks of September 11 changed his sense of responsibility and focus on his work, while causing him to review his value system. He also speaks about the necessity of serving the team as an essential career-building philosophy, rather than merely serving oneself.

What was the best piece of advice you ever received?

There are two pieces of advice, actually. One is to take complex situations and render them simple. We have a tendency to take simple situations and render them complex. Acknowledge and deal with the complexities, but try to translate all that into meaningful action.

The second piece of advice came from the former managing partner of Deloitte & Touche, Ed Kangas: God gave you two ears and one mouth for a reason. Listening, particularly in the line of work we're in, is far more important than talking. If you're going to understand a situation for all its complexities and be able to interpret and lead people, you have to first listen to understand what issues they have and their perspectives. Listen carefully and often.

What was the moment your career changed forever?

There were two points when my career changed. The first one would be the decision my wife and I made in 1983 to leave my career in higher education, or at least leave my job, and follow her career. She was vice president of Hyatt Hotel Corp., and she was actually in HR before I was. She had a career opportunity in Boston, and I had been the director of housing programs at Michigan State University in East Lansing, where I earned my master's degree and completed coursework for my doctorate. I would probably still be there, certainly still in higher education, were it not for that event. And so I said to myself, "Sue has the opportunity in Boston. There are eighty-five colleges and universities in the greater Boston area. Surely I can find a meaningful higher education position." And I did. But just as I was getting ready to accept the job, I saw an ad for a recruiting manager at Touche Ross in Boston.

What was it about that ad that spoke to you?

I knew the firm because many of my students had gone into what were then known as the Big Eight accounting firms. Recruiting college students is the other side of the equation I had just spent ten years on. So I thought, "I'll just talk to these guys. Let's see if (A) there's any interest on their part, and (B) there's any interest on *my* part." I've always been of the mind if you get thrown into circumstances, make the best of the circumstances and learn from them. I decided to follow a little bit of my own advice. It wasn't so much the ad that got to me but the response from the firm. The first conversation that I had with the person who called me from Touche Ross turned into an hour-and-a-half-long conversation. I went to visit with a number of people, and I concluded that I would regret it if I didn't do this.

What was the magical element that attracted you?

It was the people. It was their passion to do something different from what had ever been done at that time. HR was never really active in what was then known as public accounting firms. This guy, Jim McBride, wanted to change that. I was enamored of him and others I had met. I said, "If you want to change that, and it's something worth changing, I'd love to help you with it." As a recruiter, I had no designs on the current job that I have now, obviously. It was a far piece from my job as an audit recruiter in the Boston office to the chief HR officer of the firm, but that's what I did. Just that decision to follow Sue and then respond to the ad produced a wide wake.

The other moment that changed my career was the terrorist attack in New York on September 11. It affirmed my own sense of responsibility to the organization and my own sense of what I should be focusing on. It affirmed my value system, telling me to hold close what I do hold closest to me and my purpose for being here. I was at 50th and Broadway when the event began; I witnessed it and then I led the firm through it—along with a lot of other very dedicated people, I might add. I don't know if it was career- and life-changing as much as it was career- and life-*affirming*. Maybe that's a better way to say it.

You couldn't live through that, both in the moment and in the aftermath, and not have your perspective reminded or changed to where it needed to be.

What is the one thing you wish you had done differently?

To have listened better and learned more from the people who were around me than I did. I like to pride myself on doing that very thing, but every time I sit down and think what I might have done differently or what I might have thought differently, it generally comes down to the fact it was right in front of me and I didn't see it. Or maybe it would have helped if I had asked a few questions. It really comes down to taking full advantage of the people who were around me or who had been in front of me and have had that experience. It doesn't necessarily mean just seeking and listening to the counsel of elders. It's listening to the people who are all around you. That certainly was one of my experiences on September 11.

What is the best piece of advice you have to offer those on the way up?

Worry less about yourself and worry more about the work you're supposed to do and the value that it can add to the business or enterprise you're associated with. There are issues of trust associated with that, obviously, particularly in the current world we're living in. But if you do your very best work and look for ways to add value, then all the rest of the stuff falls into place. But if, on the other hand, you say, "What's in it for me and how will what they're asking me to do better advance my career?" I would argue that most of the time you'll be frustrated.

If you'd worry a little less about your current pickle and worry more about getting your business out of the pickle that it's in, you'd be in a lot better place. Businesses are dealing with increasingly complex problems. It used to be that they could isolate a problem, or a series of problems, into a particular category or place. And certainly for our clients we see that the nature of the issues that we face are far more complex—whether it's from the human side of the enterprise, the technology side of the enterprise, the multicultural aspect of business, the fact that an HR person would be called on to deal with the SARS virus, destabilization of economies, war, pestilence. You've got to have a broad-based understanding of business and a really broad understanding of how things work to find that place to add value and solve those problems.

What do up-and-comers need now that you didn't need twenty years ago?

They need to be able to find a nagging problem that the business is dealing with and then go solve it. They need good analytical skills, and they need to have knowledge of business and the drivers of the mission of that business, which is most often profit, although it might be service. And they need to understand what it is that they do that relates to enhancing those levers to make that business more successful.

Being a strategic business partner begins at the very beginning of your career. The rarified air is not reserved for the people who have put in their time. In fact, not only do you need to better understand the nature of the complex problems the business is dealing with, but you need to be able to execute and effectively implement that which you have suggested be done. There's been a long-held view that the strategic business partner no longer has to deal with the implementation and the tactical stuff. Nothing can be further from the truth. I've seen the shore littered with HR careers of people who have thought, "Okay, I've put my time in doing the tactical stuff. Now I want to go in and do strategy."

That may have been true at some point in time. It's not the case any more. You have to be able to effectively implement and lead teams that implement solutions to complex problems. And that's something that you have to learn by practicing and failing at—as well as succeeding at—very early in your career. I don't think that you can take a remedial course in that.

Many really bright people who work in human resources say, "I want to get an advanced degree; what should it be in?" And I say, "Not human resources." Take a master's in business administration. You need to be able to understand the complex environment in which you're living and supposedly dedicating yourself to serving. HR is important work, and it is a discipline, and it needs to be learned. But in terms of academic study, no. If you're in the for-profit sector, a general business administration degree is a good one.

What is the best thing new entrants can do to prepare themselves for their future careers?

Learn the business.

What is the worst thing they can do?

Become myopic and focused only on their little piece of the pie and not on the big picture. The HR profession today is not for the faint of heart. Although I think it may still be viewed that way by some, it's really quite the contrary. There are tough and scary issues that really good HR professionals who are seen as strategic business advisors are called on to deal with. Hunkering down and hoping the storm will pass—or letting the opportunities that are initially disguised as problems pass you by—is a big mistake. There are easier ways to make a living.

What do you look for when you hire a new HR person today?

Someone who is very intellectually smart but also ethically, morally, and practically grounded. Someone who plays well with others, as opposed to preferring to play by him- or herself. Someone who has a desire and some track record of experience fixing things and making things better—who understands our business or who has made an attempt to understand our business, the issues that we're dealing with and the HR implications of those issues. Someone who can demonstrate that he or she can add value to the table.

It's about leading people, it's about connecting people with each other to cause them to perform at a higher level than they would otherwise perform without you, and it's really more about helping people discover their capability within themselves, not within *you* as an HR person.

Know enough to know that you don't know enough and then give it to someone who does.

In order to be effective in dealing with people, you have to be humble. You will certainly have many opportunities to be humbled. One of the experiences I had on September 11 was what we did to respond to that situation on behalf of our people and then our clients. What I saw happen then was people rising up to meet a challenge that the average person who knew any one of those people the day before would have said, "They could never do that."

There were so many examples of singular performance at one level. But what was even more amazing to me was how all those people linked together to drive a result that was absolutely critical to the business and the people in the business. I was not conscious of that at the time, though. This kind of awareness only comes on reflection. And it was truly amazing. If we can take from that experience and move forward in a way that's better for the business and everyone in it, there are clearly some lessons there.

What risk did you take in your career that paid off?

I confronted the senior leadership of the firm. As a result, we made the right decision when we were getting ready to make the wrong decision. It paid off for the organization, and it paid off for me. I was seen as someone who would stand up to someone of greater position of authority, power, and responsibility.

But I think less about what people think of me and more about what they think of *themselves* as a result of having interacted with me. I'm a behaviorist in that I believe that people's sense of ethical self-esteem drives how they behave and what they do. The more you can ethically make people's self-esteem go up, the better off you are.

INTERVIEW

Sherry Whitely

Senior Vice President, Human Resources, Intuit

SHERRY WHITELEY FELL INTO HR as a favor. While on a completely different corporate track at Silicon Graphics, she agreed to help manage the company's project of hiring 2,500 people within a year. During that time, her co-workers noticed a different gleam in her eye and took her aside, suggesting that she consider making HR a permanent career change. From that point on, her résumé bounces all around the various functions, titles, and levels of HR, reflecting her passion for capturing and learning as much as she could about the profession.

Today she is the senior vice president of the 6,700-employee Intuit, which is best known in the consumer marketplace for its Quicken® and TurboTax® products. In this interview she talks about her philosophy of continuous learning by selecting the best teachers, mentors, and role models.

What is the best piece of advice you've ever received?

Always do what you love and what you would do even if you didn't get paid for it. A lot of people do what they do out of fear or for money. There are days that are hard and I remind myself: I love this and I would be doing it anyway.

I didn't decide I wanted to be in HR and plan for it. When I finished college, I was more prepared to be in marketing. I worked as a product marketing manager for four years and then transitioned over to the consumer side of the business, where I was a product development manager. I was then a general manager, then vice president of product development, and then I became head of desktop strategy in the IT group at Silicon

Graphics. One day the CEO and HR manager came to me and said, "We're about to add 2,500 people in a year. Would you consider being head of talent acquisition for eighteen months, just as a favor to us?"

I said okay. I cared about the company. I knew we'd be doubling the size of the company, and it would be an opportunity to make a big difference. We ended up adding 3,000 people that year. At the end of the period, they kept their promise and created a job for me in marketing. But then the head of HR had dinner with me and said, "You should rethink this. You're good in marketing, but every time you talk about any of the HR levers, you light up. You have a lot of passion for it. You really should think about a career in HR."

I had decided very early in my career that I would only take work that makes me happy and with companies where I can bring my entire self to work. This decision was challenged right away when after graduation all my friends were getting great jobs, and I was still looking. Meaning well, they kept giving me these books on how to find a job. But all those books said more or less the same thing: To get a good job, you have to hide your individuality. I finally threw them against the wall and said, "If this is what it takes to be successful, I'll just stop at wherever my career takes me because that's good enough."

And that decision freed me to be very selective. I only pick companies where my entire self can come to work every day. And that's the advice I give people: Don't try to fit into a culture but find a culture that fits you, where you can sign up and it feels right going to work every day.

What is the one thing you wish you had done differently?

I got to the point in my career where I was going to school at night studying for my MBA and hiring MBAs during the day. The pressure of work began to get really tiring and I thought, "Maybe I'm past the point where I need an MBA because I'm hiring MBAs and my work demands are so big." There are a lot of times now that I regret not finishing it. It's not that I need it as a calling card for opening doors. I just regret not finishing something. And I think the opportunity to get exposed to a lot of people in different companies and industries would have been very helpful. If I had to do it over again, I would have finished.

What is the best piece of advice you have to offer for HR professionals beginning their careers?

Don't get so hung up about the title. Focus on what you need to learn or what you want to learn. Once I decided to make a career in HR, I was already in a very senior position. So I did all sorts of craziness in order to give myself the foundation I needed for this new profession: I went from being a vice president to being a director. Then, because I wanted to do line HR, I became a senior manager for a while. Then I became a director again. After that I did a stint as manager of learning and development. I did that for about eight years, rotating to different jobs inside the company every twelve to fifteen months.

I cared a lot early on about who I worked for in HR. I picked what I wanted to learn and who I wanted to learn it from.

So that's my second piece of advice: Choose your teachers carefully. I didn't always pick the best HR person I knew but the best person at what it was I wanted to learn right then. I didn't expect them to be completely well-rounded and awesome in everything. I knew what it was I wanted their mentorship for. Don't look for an all-around HR person. They don't exist.

And pick a growing company that has a lot of opportunities for rotation, as opposed to a small company with a big title. Pick an environment where you want to come to work every day with a lot of HR opportunities that you can rotate around. It's the best way to build a strong foundation in HR.

What is the best thing new entrants can do for themselves?

You want to have lots of different role models. You'll pick up different things from different folks. Don't look for just one person to be all things for you.

What do up and coming professionals need now that you didn't need when you were starting your career?

People need to have change management acumen in a way I didn't need twenty or even ten years ago. There is so much change in market environments and the world. HR can either be behind the proverbial elephant scooping it up or they can be in the front helping the company to drive the agenda. In order to do that, you must have change management in your skill set.

There are many different change management methodologies. Pick the one that works for you. Or if you're already in a company, find out which one is being used in that environment. That way you won't have competing methodologies.

Whichever methodology you select, become an expert in it. When you're seen as an expert, then you're in a natural leadership position.

What is the worst thing new entrants can do to themselves?

You shouldn't think you have your career all figured out. You can have a rough idea, but you should be open to all the possibilities that come your way that you can't even envision at this point. I find a lot of people are closed off to opportunities because they perceive them as not being part of their plan. I spend a lot of time talking to people about their *plan,* versus the *opportunity* that has presented itself. Don't be so committed to a plan that you're not open to new opportunities or new ways of reinventing yourself.

What characteristics and qualities do you look for when hiring HR professionals for your department?

I look for integrity. It's one of those things that can't be situational. I also look for leadership skills. It's hard to coach leaders if you're not role modeling good leadership yourself. Do you walk the talk? Do you have the confidence to hire strong teams? Do you have the credibility to give advice?

I like people who love to grow and learn. Environments are changing so much, it's important to stay excited about learning and growing.

I also look for people who are good at *executing.* There are a lot of people who can talk vision and strategy, but if nothing ever gets executed then there are no points on the board at the end of the day.

A sense of humor is also essential. When people talk about my HR team, the one thing they always talk about is the fact that we laugh a lot. The other night we went out to dinner to celebrate the end of our fiscal year. The restaurant closed the door to our private dining room because we were laughing so much we were disturbing the other guests.

So my ideal HR team is one made up of individuals who perform at a high level but who don't take themselves so seriously that they can't have a good time.

What risk did you take in your career that paid off in the long run?

Over the years opportunities found me before I was done with the one I was currently working on. I was the product development manager at a game company, and the general manager position came open. Management was going to go to the outside and fill the position with a qualified, experienced general manager. I was neither of those things. But I went in to my boss anyway and said, "I would really like this job and I want to talk to you about it." He looked at me and probably thought, "Wow! I can't believe she's doing this." Remember, I'm not the kind of person who asks for money or anything I want for my career. I just always operate on the assumption that if you just work hard then the right things will happen. So he must have been shocked by my aggressiveness.

So he said, "Why should you get this job and why do you think you're qualified?"

And I said, "I know I've never done it before but I've never really failed at anything I really put my heart to, and I'll put my heart to this." Which is true.

So then he went to the CEO, who said to him, "She's not remotely qualified for this job; what are you thinking?"

My boss replied, "I come back to her reasoning that she's never failed and she'd really put her heart into this. She has delivered."

It was a big risk for me personally because of who I am. It's much easier to stay safe in a job you're qualified for and overdeliver than try this new thing. And have this first big failure on your record. I was able to make it work by hiring the very best people I could recruit to make up the rest of the team, and then learn from them.

One of the best things I tell people to do is learn how to recruit top talent. I found the best marketing person I could. I found someone who had been a general manager before. I recruited people from a competitor where they were lower in the organization and couldn't have the impact they could have by working with me. I offered them the chance to be at the table, and we'd make the decisions together and have fun. I recruited people who came because they were given a chance to play.

It took two years before I felt remotely qualified. It happened one day at a time. Confidence happens one day at a time. One day I became the vice president of all the general managers. But, you know, that took another two years.

How do you keep your passion for HR refreshed?

I read a lot. I'm one of those people who read leadership books on vacation. It's fun to think about and read about what other people are thinking and doing.

I'm also careful about who I choose to work with. I'll pick consultants I want to learn from and spend time with. They never know when they come to bid for a project that one of my key questions is whether I think I am going to enjoy spending time with them.

And, of course, I seek high performers as employees. In the last three years we've been focusing on performance and raising the bar. Critics have assumed that we're going to trade off being a great place to work in favor of higher expectations. Those aren't mutually exclusive things. You can be a great place to work and a high-performance organization at the same time. High-performing people actually want to work in a great place to work.

And as a result of all these great people I work with, I think I'm more productive. I'm really joyful when I come to work, and I have a lot of energy for what I do.

8

PREPARE YOURSELF FOR A FUTURE YOU CAN'T IMAGINE TODAY

Times are changing so rapidly that your career will unfold in ways that would surprise even the most rigorous strategic planner. This chapter provides a summary of the advice provided in this book on how to make decisions and build life and work habits that will set into motion the *opening* of doors so far into the future that you can't even imagine them today.

THROUGHOUT THIS BOOK my main message has been that you have more control over your career than you think you do. And I've been encouraging you to make your career decisions and choices with careful planning, always with your dream objectives in mind. And so together we've covered the essential steps toward building your future from your present circumstances, whatever they may be:

- Know what you want and the various skill sets and experiences that will qualify you for your ultimate dream. And then go out and make sure you get them. (See Appendix A, Career Preparation Self-Assessment.)
- Make the market come to you. Do what you can to build your recognizability factor in your community, your region, your industry, and with your peers. Network. Speak. Publish. Create innovative HR programs that capture the attention of the media. Work with your government affairs office to help your company take a leadership role in legislation.

- Understand how HR serves the business. Learn how to see what you do through your clients' eyes so you can build your credibility by helping them in truly quantifiable and meaningful ways.
- Take every opportunity to learn and grow. Welcome calculated risk.
- Don't stay too long in any one function. If you discover that you've stopped growing, look for new opportunities.
- Don't job hop. There may be times when you have no choice but to make your current position extremely short-term. Whatever you do, limit yourself to one or, at the most, two of those short stints. Remember, recruiters and search committees are looking for progressive growth and *stability.*
- Choose the people you want to learn from. Don't expect any one person to have all the answers.
- Embrace lateral moves as a form of career progression. Up is not always the best way.
- Take action to recover from your missteps. Life is long; careers are long. There is plenty of time to make a few regrettable errors. The good news is that you also have plenty of time to take corrective action.
- Expect great things from yourself. With the right plan and the right mentors, you can map your way to the future you dream of.

•

Exit Strategy: How to Break Out

All good things must come to an end. And eventually you will probably want to retire out of your corporate HR role, but still stay active, meaningful, and relevant in the next phase of your life. If you have been happy in human resources, you will want to continue to stay involved with people and organizations dedicated to creating a better future for themselves, their families, their organizations, and their community—even the profession itself.

Here is a list of a few of the many roles some HR professional friends of mine have either moved on to or retired or semi-retired *into:*

- Consultant
- Executive recruiter
- Speaker
- Author
- Teacher/College professor

- Corporate advisor or board member
- Executive coach
- Community or economic development volunteer

Just as your exit from your last company is planned out at least a year or two in advance, plan your post-career or post-retirement life in advance as well. Build your bridges now. Develop the essential relationships and skills now while you're still a powerful representative of a key corporate entity in your community. Then, as you move forward toward those years when you do not want to be 100 percent career-focused, you will have leveraged all your clout as an organizational leader and strengthened your position as an independent community leader. You can be as busy and involved as you choose to be!

•

GETTING THERE

The future is there waiting for you. And you *can* get there from wherever you are today. Just be aware that the future won't be exactly as you're envisioning it will be five, ten, or fifteen years from now. And so this is the subject of my last message to you. Prepare yourself for the future you can't even imagine.

HR has changed so much in the last thirty years, and it will continue to change in ways we can't anticipate today. The corporate world itself can shift radically. We've seen this happen repeatedly in the last fifteen years. Black Monday. September 11. April 2000, when Nasdaq took its first big tumble, pulling the dot.com boom down with it. The span of a mere twenty-four hours can cause you to throw away yesterday's plan and start with a fresh slate in the morning. As much as I encourage you to choose your career future and map your way toward it, it's also important for you to recognize that you will be rewriting your future periodically as you go.

Therefore it's not so important for you to prepare yourself for changes that you can predict as it is to keep yourself open for options all the time. This way, no matter what change happens, you will be equipped to take advantage of it. This is a lifetime of unexpected opportunities. And so one of your most important skills is to make sure you're always equipped to take advantage of them as they pop up out of the blue.

In earlier pages I've talked about *career kitting*, assembling your skills and experiences into a tote, much like the way computers are prepared for assembly at Dell. Now I'd like to invite you to consider a new concept, *career moduling.* (*Module,* by the way, is not a verb, so don't expect to find this concept in any dictionary.) Picture your career in distinct phases: Perhaps a five-year chunk doing one thing and then progressing on to a four-year stint in another area of HR, and so on. Now picture each phase, or module, as a box. In your mind's eye, make sure your career module always has at least one side open so that you can attach your next module to your current one.

It's easier said than done. If you're too rigid with your expectations for your next move, you may discover that you've shaped the opening so that only one next step can fit it, in which case, you may disqualify yourself for an option that would have been even better for you in the long run. Keeping that one side wide open and compatible with all sorts of modules will help you stay available to a wide variety of thrilling options.

Here's how you keep your career modules compatible with unexpected opportunities:

STAY CURIOUS. Stay open to and seriously consider all opportunities that present themselves, even if they show up as faint glimmerings on the horizon. You may decide eventually that you will pass up one or more of those opportunities, but you will be able to make that decision from an informed perspective.

GIVE YOURSELF THE CHANCE TO TRY NEW THINGS. You don't have to love everything you try. You don't even have to succeed. But you may surprise yourself. You'll learn a new skill, discover an income source that you hadn't anticipated, meet a new person who will introduce you to someone who will change your life.

EMBRACE FAILURE. There is value in almost every new thing that you do, even if to the outside world your adventure resulted in failure. If you learned one new thing from the experience and can use that new knowledge to carry yourself forward, then the experiment wasn't a failure.

SEIZE OPPORTUNITIES TO MEET NEW PEOPLE. As an HR careerist, you should be meeting new people all the time—*especially people outside the walls of your company.* Accept as many invitations as humanly possible. Volunteer on advisory boards. Find at least one nonprofit that dovetails with your work or your company's business. Use the Internet to meet people who can open doors for you. I had one candidate in my office a couple of weeks ago who is a graduate of Stanford University's MBA program. He was interested in an organization development position at a biotech company that is a client of mine. Before he even met with me, he jumped on-line to find out which of his fellow Stanford alumni are working at this company. And he was able to use his shared background with these people to find out more about the company and the open position.

EXPLORE UNKNOWN TERRITORY. Identify distantly related industries, companies, or professional areas and go to their conferences. If there is an opposing viewpoint to what you do or the industry you do it for, go to meetings discussing that viewpoint and try to understand the field in question from their perspective. Explore different geographic areas every year. The idea of pulling up stakes might feel completely foreign to you right now. But remember, your career is long, and your life is longer. Circumstances will change, and with that change you might have the opportunity to improve your life and prospects by moving. Don't get caught flat-footed. By exploring, you may find you're more moveable than you think you are.

GIVE YOURSELF TIME TO THINK ABOUT THE FUTURE. It's easy to put off thinking about unseen years ahead of you, especially in the face of urgent projects and the overloaded day-to-day lives we're all leading. Set aside some time on a weekly basis to focus on what opportunities the future might present to you. Think ahead, literally. When you read your local newspaper, *The Wall Street Journal,* and your professional and industry news, always ask yourself what future ramifications there might be. Where is there growth? Where is there uncertainty? Do you really believe the prognosticators? Or do you have another opinion based on your firsthand knowledge of patterns and trends? What skills do you think you'll need? Should you learn another language? Or take an assignment abroad?

In a previous chapter, I talked about how important it is to establish yourself so that the market will come to you. It's also important to establish yourself so that you'll be ready for the future, no matter what twists and turns it brings in your career.

This is an adventure of unexpected opportunities that you can't *plan* for, but that you can *prepare* yourself for.

And that's the ultimate position of strength!

SUMMARY

- Make your choices knowing that your future will be slightly—or significantly—different five, ten, or fifteen years from now.
- Build your career as a series of modular components, always with at least one open possibility that will welcome unexpected career opportunities.
- Be a lifelong learner. Stay curious. Try new things. Meet new people. Even allow yourself to fail.
- Give yourself time to think about the future. Read major daily newspapers, industry journals, and books that analyze current trends in HR and in your industry and how they may affect the face of tomorrow.

Appendix A

CAREER PREPARATION SELF-ASSESSMENT

About Career Tracks

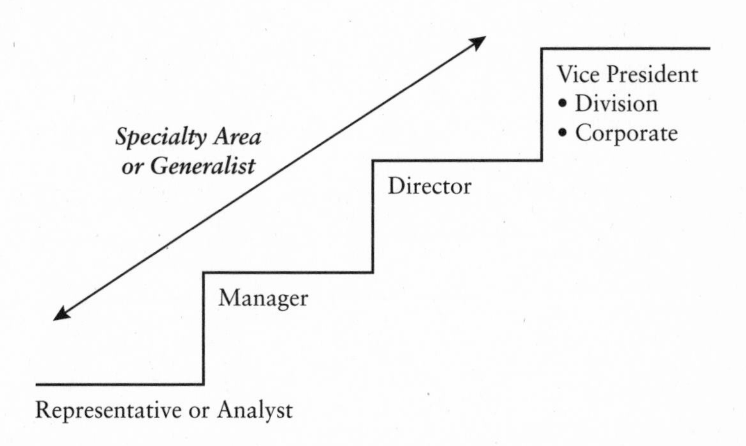

MOST CAREER TRACKS move from a representative or analyst level to manager to director. There often are multiple levels of analyst, manager, and directors within a company.

Although most senior management positions for specialty areas such as compensation, staffing, and others report to a vice president of human resources, some very large companies (>10,000 employees) have vice-presidential levels for some of the specialty areas. Also in very large companies, the senior human resources management position responsible for a substantial division or subsidiary may also be at a vice-presidential level.

About Preparation

Preparation + Opportunity = Success

On the following pages are self-assessment forms for specific skills and experiences that are typical for each of the human resources specialty and generalist areas. These forms are not intended to be all-inclusive. Nor is it necessary to be able to check off every single box on the list to grow your career. The intent is to give you a tool to help you realistically evaluate your own personal level of preparation.

If you desire to grow your career beyond where it may be at this time, it may be best to focus on areas where you have a 1, 2, or 3 rating. If you have a 4 or 5 rating in a particular area, although you may still need to stay current on the latest developments, it may not be necessary to seek out additional training in this area.

Vice President of Human Resources

1 = No Knowledge/Experience 2 = Some Knowledge 3 = Knowledge & Some Experience
4 = Good Knowledge/Experience 5 = In-depth Knowledge/Experience

Job Description: Responsible for the development and implementation of the human resources strategy for an organization and for management of a full range of human resources functions—organization development, staffing, compensation, benefits, HRIT, and generalist roles—and initiatives. This is an executive-level position and assumes an incumbent would have solid depth and breadth of human resources technical and management experience.

BASIC

___ Responsible for the full breadth of human resources functions for a corporate entity, or
___ Responsible for the full breadth of human resources functions in an autonomous division or subsidiary of a large company (typically >5,000 employees), or
___ Responsible for the full breadth of human resources functions in a significant business unit of a large company (typically >5,000 employees)
___ Selects, develops, and evaluates teams of human resources professionals that include senior management of HR specialty functions and generalists groups
___ Clearly understands and can communicate the impact of business decisions on the P&L (profit and loss) statement

Depth and Breadth of Experience typically include:

___ Organization Development
___ Staffing
___ Compensation and Benefits
___ Employee Relations and/or Labor Relations

International:

___ Europe
___ Asia
___ The Americas

Mergers, Acquisitions, and Divestitures:

___ Due Diligence
___ Integration or Transitions

ADVANCED

___ Responsible for the full breadth of human resources functions in a large company, typically >5,000 employees
___ Scope of responsibility typically involves highly complex organizations with multiple locations globally, multiple businesses, and complex corporate structures requiring extensive business knowledge
___ Interfaces with the Board of Directors on a variety of complex issues of a highly sensitive nature

MANAGEMENT

___ Responsible for development and implementation of the company's human resources strategy
___ Responsible for development and management of budgets
___ Manages the full range of human resources functions

CAREER TRACK

- May report to a division or subsidiary president or general manager
- Corporate position typically reports to a chief operating officer or a chief executive officer
- Career development may be more about personal growth, diversity of industry experience, or size or status of company

Human Resources Director

1 = No Knowledge/Experience 2 = Some Knowledge 3 = Knowledge & Some Experience
4 = Good Knowledge/Experience 5 = In-depth Knowledge/Experience

Job Description: Advises company management in policy and program matters, making or recommending appropriate decisions as consistent with strategic direction.

BASIC

___ Performs a wide variety of generalist functions in small to mid-sized companies (typically <5,000 employees), or

___ Performs a wide variety of generalist functions in larger companies for a client group or division typically consisting of <5,000 employees, or

___ Manages the full depth and breadth of the human resources function—organization development, staffing, compensation, benefits, HRIT, and generalist roles—in small companies, typically <1,000 employees

___ Selects, develops, and evaluates human resources professionals, providing support to a client group or groups within an organization

___ Assures compliance with federal and state regulations

ADVANCED

___ Clearly understands and can communicate the impact of business decisions on the P&L (profit and loss) statement

International:

- ___ Europe
- ___ Asia
- ___ The Americas

Mergers, Acquisitions, and Divestitures:

- ___ Due Diligence
- ___ Integration or Transitions

___ May interface with the Board of Directors on a variety of complex issues of a highly sensitive nature

MANAGEMENT

___ Responsible for implementation of the company's human resources strategy and plans

___ Responsible for development and management of budgets

___ Manages a staff of HR generalists responsible for delivering services to a variety of client groups within an organization

CAREER TRACK

- Typically reports to a vice president of human resources; may also report to a functional or business unit, division, or subsidiary executive
- In smaller companies (typically <1,000 employees), position may report to a chief executive officer (CEO), chief operating officer (COO), chief administrative officer (CAO) or a chief financial officer (CFO)
- To achieve a vice president of human resources role, incumbent may need to diversify experience, consider moving into a human resources specialty area, or obtaining experience in a larger company

Human Resources Generalist

(Could also be titled HR Manager, HR Director, HR Consultant, or HR Business Partner—generally an individual contributor role)

1 = No Knowledge/Experience 2 = Some Knowledge 3 = Knowledge & Some Experience
4 = Good Knowledge/Experience 5 = In-depth Knowledge/Experience

Job Description: Guides managers in the implementation of corporate polices and programs for an assigned client group; may be a department, function, business unit, or division of a large corporation.

BASIC

___ Assists senior managers in the development of solutions to organizational problems
___ Develops and/or drives company programs and initiatives
___ Handles day-to-day employee-management issues resolving conflict
___ Coaches managers in the handling of a variety of employee-management matters
___ Assures staffing requirements are met either by managing recruiters directly or working with the corporate staffing function
___ Handles implementation of human resources programs, including rollout of compensation and benefit programs, training programs, and other initiatives

ADVANCED

___ Partnered with a senior line executive, provides guidance and advise on business issues, with particular focus on people management
___ Clearly understands and can communicate the impact of business decisions on the P&L (profit and loss) statement
___ Conducts complex investigations of a litigious nature
___ Working with attorneys, resolves legal actions by either negotiating settlement or litigation minimizing impact on employer
___ Handles complex government inquiries with potential for significant negative impact, either financial or image
___ Handles international human resources matters by working with executives and work councils in a variety of countries

International:
___ Europe
___ Asia
___ The Americas

Mergers, Acquisitions, and Divestitures:
___ Due Diligence
___ Integration or Transitions

MANAGEMENT

___ May manage more junior human resources generalists responsible for delivering human resources services to a smaller subgroup of clients within assigned client group

CAREER TRACK

- Typically reports to a director or vice president of human resources
- To achieve a vice president of human resources role, incumbent may need to diversify experience, consider moving into another human resources specialty area or human resources generalist role

Staffing Professional

1 = No Knowledge/Experience 2 = Some Knowledge 3 = Knowledge & Some Experience
4 = Good Knowledge/Experience 5 = In-depth Knowledge/Experience

Job Description: Responsible for assuring staffing objectives and plans are met.

BASIC

___ Searches résumé database to identify candidates
___ Handles recruitment administration, that is, scheduling of interviews, preparation of offers, bringing people on-board, or new-hire orientations
___ Reviews résumés and conducts pre-screen interviews
___ Manages interview feedback and pre-closes or presents offers to candidates
___ Oversees the acquisition of temporary staff, typically through the use of vendors
___ Assures staffing practices are in compliance with federal and state regulations

ADVANCED

___ Develops and implements recruitment plans
___ Designs recruitment processes and policies
___ Negotiates and maintains contracts with recruiting sources such as job fairs, employment agencies, and job search websites
___ Develops and manages a variety of recruitment programs:
  ___ College relations and recruiting
  ___ Job fairs
  ___ Employee referral programs
  ___ Staffing open houses
  ___ Advertising and promotion
  ___ Staffing website
  ___ Immigration
  ___ Relocation

MANAGEMENT

___ Responsible for development and management of recruitment budgets
___ Manages a small team of recruiters and support staff to achieve staffing plans for a small to mid-sized organization (<1,000 employees)
___ Manages a complex staffing organization responsible for nationwide recruitment for multiple sites
___ Manages a complex staffing organization responsible for development and implementation of global staffing plans

CAREER TRACK

- Typically reports to a director or vice president of human resources
- To achieve a vice president of human resources role, incumbent may need to diversify experience, consider moving into another human resources specialty area or human resources generalist role

Organization Development Professional

1 = No Knowledge/Experience 2 = Some Knowledge 3 = Knowledge & Some Experience
4 = Good Knowledge/Experience 5 = In-depth Knowledge/Experience

Job Description: Consults with management to address root causes of organizational issues. Assists in the development and implementation of solutions to organizational and cultural issues.

BASIC

___ Team building
___ Meeting planning and facilitation
___ Management coaching

ADVANCED

___ Formal organization assessments
___ Culture transformation
___ Competency profiling assessment and analysis
___ Develops and/or manages succession planning programs
___ Executive coaching
___ Designs and implements interventions
___ Develops and manages executive strategy meetings
___ Large-scale change management

MANAGEMENT

___ Manages projects involving a high degree of influence and collaboration skills
___ Manages team of organization development experts (either internal professionals or external consultants) responsible for delivery of organization development services to various client groups within the organization

CAREER TRACK

- Senior individual contributor or management positions may report to a vice president of human resources or directly to a general manager of a division or subsidiary of large company; occasionally reports to the chief executive officer
- To achieve a vice president of human resources role, incumbent may need to diversify experience, consider moving into another human resources specialty area or human resources generalist role

Training or Learning and Development Professional

1 = No Knowledge/Experience 2 = Some Knowledge 3 = Knowledge & Some Experience
4 = Good Knowledge/Experience 5 = In-depth Knowledge/Experience

Job Description: Responsible for the design, preparation. and delivery of training and development programs for company managers and employees.

BASIC

___ Handles needs assessment
___ Stand-up training (certified on DDI, Zenger Miller, Performax, Wilson Learning, or other pre-developed management programs)
___ Develops and/or approves content, methods, and materials for training programs
___ Designs and conducts basic manager and employee training programs

ADVANCED

___ Designs complex management programs; may work with outside consultants or conduct portions of training personally
___ Develops succession planning programs
___ Develops executive development programs

MANAGEMENT

___ Manages projects from design through implementation
___ Project manages development and implementation of training programs and/or succession planning and executive development programs
___ Manages a variety of vendors delivering training services to the organization
___ Manages curriculum developers and trainers (may be staff or vendors), providing training programs and services to the organization
___ Manages corporate university
___ Responsible for development and management of training budgets

CAREER TRACK

- Most senior management position; typically reports to a vice president of human resources
- To achieve a vice president of human resources role, incumbent may need to diversify experience, consider moving into another human resources specialty area or human resources generalist role

Compensation Professional

1 = No Knowledge/Experience 2 = Some Knowledge 3 = Knowledge & Some Experience
4 = Good Knowledge/Experience 5 = In-depth Knowledge/Experience

Job Description: Responsible for the design, installation, and administration of pay plans and programs.

BASIC

___ Job analysis and job descriptions
___ Salary survey input
___ Market analysis of pay practices
___ Salary ranges and structures
___ Salary budgets
___ Performance management systems
___ Merit pay programs
___ Assures compliance with federal and state laws and regulations
___ Working knowledge of HRIT

ADVANCED

___ Variable (incentive/bonus) pay programs
___ Sales commission programs
___ Profit sharing/Gain sharing plans
___ Employee stock purchase plans
___ Stock option programs
Executive Compensation:
  ___ Salary and bonus
  ___ Equity (stock options, restricted stock, SARs)
  ___ Deferred compensation programs
  ___ Perks
International Compensation:
  ___ Europe
  ___ Asia
  ___ The Americas
___ Mergers and acquisitions (integration work)
___ SEC reporting and other regulatory compliance
___ Interfaces with the board of directors on complex compensation issues of a highly sensitive nature, such as executive compensation programs
___ Clearly understands and can communicate the impact of business decisions on the P&L (profit and loss) statement

MANAGEMENT

___ Project manages development and implementation of new programs
___ Prepares policies and procedures to ensure the achievement of equitable and competitive employee compensation
___ Manages a variety of vendors, including compensation consultants, third-party administrators, and outsourced administrative services
___ Manages a team of compensation analysts and administrators responsible for employee and vendor communications and administration of programs

CAREER TRACK

- Although most senior management positions typically report to a vice president of HR, may work with the senior executive team and compensation committee of the board of directors on corporate compensation strategy and executive compensation matters
- To achieve a vice president of human resources role, incumbent may need to diversify experience, consider moving into another human resources specialty area or human resources generalist role

Benefits Professional

1 = No Knowledge/Experience 2 = Some Knowledge 3 = Knowledge & Some Experience
4 = Good Knowledge/Experience 5 = In-depth Knowledge/Experience

Job Description: Responsible for the design, installation, and administration of employee benefits programs.

BASIC

___ Vacation, paid time off, leaves of absence, and unemployment insurance
___ Health insurance plans (medical, dental, life/AD&D, vision, and others)
___ Short-term and long-term disability plans
___ Section 125 plans (pre-tax premium, health care, and dependent care accounts)
___ Workers' Compensation
___ 401(k) plans
___ Working knowledge of HRIT

ADVANCED

___ Complex cafeteria or flexible benefit programs
___ Retirement programs (defined benefit and defined contribution)
___ Executive benefits (non-qualified)
Mergers and Acquisitions:
  ___ Due Diligence
  ___ Integration
International:
  ___ Europe
  ___ Asia
  ___ The Americas
___ Clearly understands and can communicate the impact of business decisions on the P&L (profit and loss) statement

MANAGEMENT

___ Manages development and implementation of new programs
___ Negotiates coverage, services, and costs with carriers and brokers
___ Manages a variety of vendors, including benefits brokers, third-party administrators, and outsourced administrative services
___ Manages a team of benefits professionals and administrators responsible for employee and vendor communications and administration of various benefit plans

CAREER TRACK

- Most senior management positions typically report to either a compensation director or a vice president of human resources
- Develop breadth of skills by acquiring experience in compensation and/or HRIT (Human Resource Information Technology)
- To achieve a vice president of human resources role, incumbent may need to diversify experience, consider moving into another human resources specialty area or human resources generalist role

Employee Relations Professional

1 = No Knowledge/Experience 2 = Some Knowledge 3 = Knowledge & Some Experience
4 = Good Knowledge/Experience 5 = In-depth Knowledge/Experience

Job Description: Responsible for addressing and resolving employee issues in the workplace.

BASIC

___ Interprets and implements company policies
___ Resolves day-to-day employee/management conflicts
___ Conducts workplace investigations of a sensitive nature
___ Responsible for routine employee communications
___ Responds to a variety of government inquiries, such as unemployment and discrimination claims

ADVANCED

___ Conducts complex workplace investigations of a litigious nature
___ Working with attorneys, resolves legal actions by either negotiating settlement or litigation minimizing impact on employer
___ Handles complex government inquiries with potential for significant negative impact on the company, either financial or image
___ Handles international employee relations matters by working with company management and local work councils in a variety of countries

International:

___ Europe
___ Asia
___ The Americas

MANAGEMENT

___ Develops or modifies policies and assures equitable implementation
___ Manages a team of employee relations experts, typically assigned to various client groups within an organization

CAREER TRACK

- Typically reports to a director or vice president of human resources
- To achieve a vice president of human resources role, incumbent may need to diversify experience, consider moving into another human resources specialty area or human resources generalist role

Labor Relations Professional

1 = No Knowledge/Experience 2 = Some Knowledge 3 = Knowledge & Some Experience
4 = Good Knowledge/Experience 5 = In-depth Knowledge/Experience

Job Description: Responsible for addressing and resolving employee issues in the workplace involving employees covered by union contracts.

BASIC

___ Interprets and implements policies within parameters of union contracts
___ Resolves day-to-day employee grievances working within the boundaries of labor contracts
___ Conducts workplace investigations of a sensitive nature
___ Responsible for routine employee and labor union communications
___ Responds to a variety of government inquiries, such as unemployment and discrimination claims

ADVANCED

___ Negotiates resolution of complex employee/management issues with union representatives
___ Conducts complex investigations of a litigious nature
___ Working with attorneys, resolves legal actions by either negotiating settlement or litigation minimizing impact on employer
___ Handles complex government inquiries with potential for significant negative impact on the company, either financial or image

MANAGEMENT

___ Part of the management team responsible for negotiating union contracts
___ Manages a team of labor relations professionals typically assigned to various client groups within an organization
___ Responsible for long-range union/management strategy; leads company's union negotiating efforts

CAREER TRACK

- Typically reports to a director or vice president of human resources
- To achieve a vice president of human resources role, incumbent may need to diversify experience, consider moving into another human resources specialty area or human resources generalist role

Other Human Resources Specialties

1 = No Knowledge/Experience 2 = Some Knowledge 3 = Knowledge & Some Experience
4 = Good Knowledge/Experience 5 = In-depth Knowledge/Experience

There are several other areas of specialization within human resources that should be mentioned.

__ HUMAN RESOURCES OPERATIONS.

This is generally a management position responsible for overseeing the administration of (but not necessarily the design aspects, although they may be included) a variety of human resources functions, such as compensation and benefits plans, stock programs, human resources call centers, registration of employees in company training programs, and so forth.

__ HUMAN RESOURCES CALL CENTERS.

Positions typically handle a variety of employee queries over the telephone. Responses often cover interpretation or communication of company policies, dissemination of information regarding payroll status, benefits, and so on. Some call centers also handle employee relations issues of a general nature; complex issues are often escalated to human resources generalists or managers for resolution.

__ DIVERSITY.

This position is generally focused on helping the company develop an environment and culture that enable it to attract and retain employees of diverse backgrounds and cultures. Position may also be responsible for development and implementation of affirmative action programs.

__ HRIT (HUMAN RESOURCES INFORMATION TECHNOLOGY).

Positions in this area are very similar to information technology positions (programmers, analysts, and so on) in other areas of the company, except that they specialize in providing systems specifically for managing employee information:

- ABRA (or other small systems typically used by companies with <1,000 employees)
- PeopleSoft
- Oracle
- SAP
- Website development (HMTL)

Appendix B

CERTIFICATIONS, TOOLS, TRAINING, AND ASSOCIATIONS

Preparation + Opportunity = Success

More About Preparation

As in nearly all professions today, a bachelor's degree is considered a minimum requirement. No amount of training or certification will replace a degree. Training and certifications are supplements to a solid educational background.

Many colleges and universities are offering bachelor's and master's degrees in human resources today. In addition, many offer degree programs designed for working professionals. Although you may know someone or even be someone who has been successful in the field without a degree, it is becoming more difficult to do so. Take a look at the programs offered by universities and colleges in your local area. In addition, some very good universities and colleges, such as the Fielding Institute, are offering degree programs on-line.

Frequently Asked Questions

If I decide to get my master's, should I get it in human resources?

I want to apologize to the profession, in advance, for my answer. A master's in human resources or organization development is great. However, if you aspire to one day be a vice president of human resources, I would encourage you to pursue an MBA (master's in business administration). The most sought-after degree at the executive level is an MBA.

For those of you who want to specialize in organization development, a master's is often considered a minimum requirement. A Ph.D. is not uncommon. The more education in this area, the better.

Does it matter what school I graduate from?

Yes, but. Yes, the higher the rating of the school the better. But given whatever your personal limitations may be, you would be better to get a degree from a B or C school than to procrastinate because the A school may be out of your reach. Over time and backed up with great experience, the actual major of your degree and the rating of the school become less important.

I am already forty years old. Is it too late for me to get a degree?

It is never too late. You could be working for another twenty-five years. Do all that you can to assure your employability.

Certifications

Many of the organizations listed below offer a variety of certifications and tools; we have listed only the most common. Additional information can be found on the websites.

HUMAN RESOURCES

- HR Strategy and Practice, The Human Resource Planning Society, www.hrps.org
- Senior HR Practitioner, The Human Resource Planning Society, www.hrps.org
- PHR (Professional in Human Resources), Society for Human Resource Management (SHRM), www.shrm.org
- SPHR (Senior Professional in Human Resources), Society for Human Resource Management (SHRM), www.shrm.org

STAFFING

- CIR (Certified Internet Recruiter), AIRS Human Capital Solutions, www.airsdirectory.com
- CDR (Certified Diversity Recruiter), AIRS Human Capital Solutions, www.airsdirectory.com

COMPENSATION AND BENEFITS

- CMS (Compensation Management Specialist), International Society of Certified Employee Benefits Specialists, www.iscebs.org
- RPA (Retirement Plan Associate), International Society of Certified Employee Benefits Specialists, www.iscebs.org
- CEBS (Certified Employee Benefits Specialist), International Society of Certified Employee Benefits Specialists, www.iscebs.org
- CEPI (Certified Equity Professional Institute), International Society of Certified Employee Benefits Specialists, www.iscebs.org
- GBA (Group Benefits Associate), International Society of Certified Employee Benefits Specialists, www.iscebs.org
- CCP (Certified Compensation Professional), World at Work, www.worldatwork.org

- CBP (Certified Benefits Professional), World at Work, www.worldatwork.org
- GRP (Global Remuneration Professional), World at Work, www.worldatwork.org

Some Widely Used Tools and Training Programs

Many of the organizations listed below offer a variety of certifications and tools; we have just listed the most common. Additional information can be found on the websites.

TOOLS

- DiSC Profiles, Carlson Learning Company, www.hughesconsultinggrp.com
- Dimensions of Leadership, Performax Systems, www.performax2000.com
- MBTI (Myers-Briggs Type Indicator), www.cpp.com
- Benchmarks (360-degree feedback), Center for Creative Leadership, www.ccl.org
- Executive Dimensions (360-degree feedback for executives), Center for Creative Leadership, www.ccl.org

TRAINING PROGRAMS

- Leading Organizational Transition, William Bridges & Associates, www.wmbridges.com
- 7 Habits of Highly Effective People®, Franklin Covey, www.franklincovey.com
- Situational Leadership, The Ken Blanchard Companies, www.kenblanchard.com or Center for Leadership Studies, www.situation.com
- Targeted Selection, DDI (Development Dimensions International, Inc.), www.ddi.com
- The Voices 360-Degree Feedback, Lominger Ltd., www.lominger.com
- Organization Development, NTL Institute, www.ntl.org
- Change Management Leadership, NTL Institute, www.ntl.org
- Diversity Management, NTL Institute, www.ntl.org
- Experienced-Based Learning and Training, NTL Institute, www.ntl.org
- Strategic Human Resources Planning, University of Michigan, www.bus.umich.edu

- Human Resource Executive Program, University of Michigan, www.bus.umich.edu
- Advanced Human Resource Executive Program, University of Michigan, www.bus.umich.edu
- Interviewing: A Strategic Approach, University of Michigan, www.bus.umich.edu
- Negotiating and Administering the Labor Contract, University of Michigan, www.bus.umich.edu
- Strategic Collective Bargaining, University of Michigan, www.bus.umich.edu

Associations

This list is not all-inclusive. These are nationally recognized organizations. There are often local associations that are just too numerous to list. Additional information can be found on the websites.

- American Council on International Personnel, www.acip.com
- American Society for Healthcare Human Resources Administration, www.hospitalconnect.com/DesktopServlet
- ASTD (American Society for Training and Development), www.astd.org
- College and University Professional Association for Human Resources, www.cupahr.org/
- Employee Benefits Research Institute, www.ebri.org
- HRPS (Human Resources Planning Society), www.hrps.org
- IHRIM (International Human Resources Information Management), www.ihrim.org
- International Foundation of Employee Benefits, www.ifebp.org
- International Public Management Association for Human Resources, www.ipma-hr.org
- National Association for Healthcare Recruitment, www.nahcr.com
- SHRM (Society for Human Resources Management), www.shrm.org/
- World at Work (formerly American Compensation Association), www.worldatwork.org

INDEX

D

E

ABOUT THE AUTHORS

JEANNE PALMER (San Jose, California) is one of the few executive recruiters specializing exclusively in the human resource management field. She is the founder of The Palmer Advantage. Her background includes more than twenty years of HR management experience in Fortune 500 (Raytheon, Teledyne, and Western Digital) and start-up technology companies, followed by ten years managing HR consulting firms.

Ms. Palmer manages the University of California-Santa Cruz Extension's HR Management Program and is an advisory board member of San Jose State University's HR degree program. She is also an officer of HR, Inc., an organization dedicated to the betterment of the profession by funding scholarships for HR majors, and Project HIRED, a nonprofit organization helping people with disabilities obtain meaningful employment; an advisory board member of Unicru Corporation; and a frequent speaker for numerous HR associations, including the Northern California Human Resources Association and the Silicon Valley Compensation Association. She has appeared on *CBS Marketwatch* and is often quoted by the *San Jose Mercury News* and the *San Francisco Chronicle*. She can be contacted at jpalmer@palmeradv.com.

MARTHA I. FINNEY (Los Gatos, California) is a business journalist and consultant specializing in leadership communications, publishing, and employee engagement. The author or ghostwriter of nine books, she is also the producer of the web-based journal *Working From the Heart-Land,* which was featured on NPR's *Morning Edition* and CNN's *Voices of America* series. She is also a regular columnist for *HR Innovator* magazine. Her latest book was *HR from the Heart: Inspir-ing Stories and Strategies for Building the People Side of Great Business,* which she wrote with Libby Sartain, Chief People Officer at Yahoo! She can be contacted at Martha@marthafinney.com.

ABOUT THE AUTHOR

Pfeiffer Publications Guide

This guide is designed to familiarize you with the various types of Pfeiffer publications. The formats section describes the various types of products that we publish; the methodologies section describes the many different ways that content might be provided within a product. We also provide a list of the topic areas in which we publish.

FORMATS

In addition to its extensive book-publishing program, Pfeiffer offers content in an array of formats, from fieldbooks for the practitioner to complete, ready-to-use training packages that support group learning.

FIELDBOOK Designed to provide information and guidance to practitioners in the midst of action. Most fieldbooks are companions to another, sometimes earlier, work, from which its ideas are derived; the fieldbook makes practical what was theoretical in the original text. Fieldbooks can certainly be read from cover to cover. More likely, though, you'll find yourself bouncing around following a particular theme, or dipping in as the mood, and the situation, dictate.

HANDBOOK A contributed volume of work on a single topic, comprising an eclectic mix of ideas, case studies, and best practices sourced by practitioners and experts in the field.

An editor or team of editors usually is appointed to seek out contributors and to evaluate content for relevance to the topic. Think of a handbook not as a ready-to-eat meal, but as a cookbook of ingredients that enables you to create the most fitting experience for the occasion.

RESOURCE Materials designed to support group learning. They come in many forms: a complete, ready-to-use exercise (such as a game); a comprehensive resource on one topic (such as conflict management) containing a variety of methods and approaches; or a collection of like-minded activities (such as icebreakers) on multiple subjects and situations.

TRAINING PACKAGE An entire, ready-to-use learning program that focuses on a particular topic or skill. All packages comprise a guide for the facilitator/trainer and a workbook for the participants. Some packages are supported with additional media—such as video—or learning aids, instruments, or other devices to help participants understand concepts or practice and develop skills.

- *Facilitator/trainer's guide* Contains an introduction to the program, advice on how to organize and facilitate the learning event, and step-by-step instructor notes. The guide also contains copies of presentation materials—handouts, presentations, and overhead designs, for example—used in the program.
- *Participant's workbook* Contains exercises and reading materials that support the learning goal and serves as a valuable reference and support guide for participants in the weeks and months that follow the learning event. Typically, each participant will require his or her own workbook.

ELECTRONIC CD-ROMs and web-based products transform static Pfeiffer content into dynamic, interactive experiences. Designed to take advantage of the searchability, automation, and ease-of-use that technology provides, our e-products bring convenience and immediate accessibility to your workspace.

METHODOLOGIES

CASE STUDY A presentation, in narrative form, of an actual event that has occurred inside an organization. Case studies are not prescriptive, nor are they used to prove a point; they are designed to develop critical analysis and decision-making skills. A case study has a specific time frame, specifies a sequence of events, is narrative in structure, and contains a plot structure—an issue (what should be/have been done?). Use case studies when the goal is to enable participants to apply previously learned theories to the circumstances in the case, decide what is pertinent, identify the real issues, decide what should have been done, and develop a plan of action.

ENERGIZER A short activity that develops readiness for the next session or learning event. Energizers are most commonly used after a break or lunch to stimulate or refocus the group. Many involve some form of physical activity, so they are a useful way to counter post-lunch lethargy. Other uses include transitioning from one topic to another, where "mental" distancing is important.

EXPERIENTIAL LEARNING ACTIVITY (ELA) A facilitator-led intervention that moves participants through the learning cycle from experience to application (also known as a Structured Experience). ELAs are carefully thought-out designs in which there is a definite learning purpose and intended outcome. Each step—everything that participants do during the activity—facilitates the accomplishment of the stated goal. Each ELA includes complete instructions for facilitating the intervention and a clear statement of goals, suggested group size and timing, materials required, an explanation of the process, and, where appropriate, possible variations to the activity. (For more detail on Experiential Learning Activities, see the Introduction to the *Reference Guide to Handbooks and Annuals*, 1999 edition, Pfeiffer, San Francisco.)

GAME A group activity that has the purpose of fostering team spirit and togetherness in addition to the achievement of a pre-stated goal. Usually contrived—undertaking a desert expedition, for example—this type of learning method offers an engaging means for participants to demonstrate and practice business and interpersonal skills. Games are effective for team building and personal development mainly because the goal is subordinate to the process—the means through which participants reach decisions, collaborate, communicate, and generate trust and understanding. Games often engage teams in "friendly" competition.

ICEBREAKER A (usually) short activity designed to help participants overcome initial anxiety in a training session and/or to acquaint the participants with one another. An icebreaker can be a fun activity or can be tied to specific topics or training goals. While a useful tool in itself, the icebreaker comes into its own in situations where tension or resistance exists within a group.

INSTRUMENT A device used to assess, appraise, evaluate, describe, classify, and summarize various aspects of human behavior. The term used to describe an instrument depends primarily on its format and purpose. These terms include survey, questionnaire, inventory, diagnostic, survey, and poll. Some uses of instruments include providing instrumental feedback to group members, studying here-and-now processes or functioning within a group, manipulating group composition, and evaluating outcomes of training and other interventions.

Instruments are popular in the training and HR field because, in general, more growth can occur if an individual is provided with a method for focusing specifically on his or her own behavior. Instruments also are used to obtain information that will serve as a basis for change and to assist in workforce planning efforts.

Paper-and-pencil tests still dominate the instrument landscape with a typical package comprising a facilitator's guide, which offers advice on administering the instrument and interpreting the collected data, and an initial set of instruments. Additional instruments are available separately. Pfeiffer, though, is investing heavily in e-instruments. Electronic instrumentation provides effortless distribution and, for larger groups particularly, offers advantages over paper-and-pencil tests in the time it takes to analyze data and provide feedback.

LECTURETTE A short talk that provides an explanation of a principle, model, or process that is pertinent to the participants' current learning needs. A lecturette is intended to establish a common language bond between the trainer and the participants by providing a mutual frame of reference. Use a lecturette as an introduction to a group activity or event, as an interjection during an event, or as a handout.

MODEL A graphic depiction of a system or process and the relationship among its elements. Models provide a frame of reference and something more tangible, and more easily remembered, than a verbal explanation. They also give participants something to "go on," enabling them to track their own progress as they experience the dynamics, processes, and relationships being depicted in the model.

ROLE PLAY A technique in which people assume a role in a situation/scenario: a customer service rep in an angry-customer exchange, for example. The way in which the role is approached is then discussed and feedback is offered. The role play is often repeated using a different approach and/or incorporating changes made based on feedback received. In other words, role playing is a spontaneous interaction involving realistic behavior under artificial (and safe) conditions.

SIMULATION A methodology for understanding the interrelationships among components of a system or process. Simulations differ from games in that they test or use a model that depicts or mirrors some aspect of reality in form, if not necessarily in content. Learning occurs by studying the effects of change on one or more factors of the model. Simulations are commonly used to test hypotheses about what happens in a system—often referred to as "what if?" analysis—or to examine best-case/worst-case scenarios.

THEORY A presentation of an idea from a conjectural perspective. Theories are useful because they encourage us to examine behavior and phenomena through a different lens.

TOPICS

The twin goals of providing effective and practical solutions for workforce training and organization development and meeting the educational needs of training and human resource professionals shape Pfeiffer's publishing program. Core topics include the following:

Leadership & Management
Communication & Presentation
Coaching & Mentoring
Training & Development
E-Learning
Teams & Collaboration
OD & Strategic Planning
Human Resources
Consulting

Customer Care

Have a question, comment, or suggestion? Contact us! We value your feedback and we want to hear from you.

For questions about this or other Pfeiffer products, you may contact us by:

E-mail: **customer@wiley.com**

Mail: **Customer Care Wiley/Pfeiffer**
10475 Crosspoint Blvd.
Indianapolis, IN 46256

Phone: **(US) 800-274-4434** (Outside the US: 317-572-3985)

Fax: **(US) 800-569-0443** (Outside the US: 317-572-4002)

To order additional copies of this title or to browse other Pfeiffer products, visit us online at **www.pfeiffer.com**.

For **Technical Support** questions call **(800) 274-4434.**

For authors guidelines, log on to www.pfeiffer.com and click on "Resources for Authors."

If you are . . .

A **college bookstore, a professor, an instructor, or work in higher education** and you'd like to place an order or request an exam copy, please contact jbreview@wiley.com.

A **general retail bookseller** and you'd like to establish an account or speak to a local sales representative, contact Melissa Grecco at 201-748-6267 or mgrecco@wiley.com.

An **exclusively on-line bookseller**, contact Amy Blanchard at 530-756-9456 or ablanchard@wiley.com or Jennifer Johnson at 206-568-3883 or jjohnson@wiley.com, both of our Online Sales department.

A **librarian or library representative**, contact John Chambers in our Library Sales department at 201-748-6291 or jchamber@wiley.com.

A **reseller, training company/consultant, or corporate trainer**, contact Charles Regan in our Special Sales department at 201-748-6553 or cregan@wiley.com.

A **specialty retail distributor** (includes specialty gift stores, museum shops, and corporate bulk sales), contact Kim Hendrickson in our Special Sales department at 201-748-6037 or khendric@wiley.com.

Purchasing for the **Federal government**, contact Ron Cunningham in our Special Sales department at 317-572-3053 or rcunning@wiley.com.

Purchasing for a **State or Local government**, contact Charles Regan in our Special Sales department at 201-748-6553 or cregan@wiley.com.